ETHICAL INVESTMENT
A SAVER'S GUIDE

ETHICAL INVESTMENT

A SAVER'S GUIDE

Peter Lang

JON CARPENTER

First published in 1996 by Jon Carpenter Publishing
The Spendlove Centre, Charlbury, Oxfordshire OX7 3PQ (01608 811969)

© Peter Lang, 1996

ISBN 1 897766 20 3

Printed and bound in England by J.W. Arrowsmith Ltd, Bristol

To Gerald and Lily

Caveat

● ●

Nothing in the book should be interpreted as advice or a recommen-
dation to buy or sell any securities. Readers are warned that the prices
of shares, unit trusts, and bank and building society interest rates, can
fall as well as rise and that past performance is no reliable guide to
what may happen in the future. The author and publishers can take no
responsibility for any investment decisions taken by readers as a result
of reading this book. All investors are advised to ascertain for themselves the charging mechanisms, future prospects and degree of risk to
be found in any investments whether described in this book or not.
Only appropriately licensed financial advisers are allowed to advise
you on your choice, and this book does not claim to be a substitute for
such advice.

The information given about particular funds, companies or other
organisations is as accurate as we can make it at the time of publication, but readers should obtain up to date information for themselves
before making any investment decision.

Contents

Preface

●●●

" RABBI SOLOMON HAD never owned a house or saved any money, but one of his greatest pleasures was to travel. On one sea journey his fellow passengers were wealthy merchants who one night were boasting about what they owned and how much their goods were worth.

Eventually the merchants turned to the Rabbi, thinking he was also a merchant. 'What goods do you have to sell and how much are they worth?' they inquired.

'My goods are more valuable than all the rest of your goods put together,' replied Rabbi Solomon mysteriously. The merchants were astonished at this and demanded: 'What are your goods? Why are they more valuable than ours?' But the rabbi said nothing and the merchants began to mock him: 'You're lying to us. You don't have anything of real value. In fact you probably own nothing more than the clothes you stand up in.'

Three days later the ship was attacked by pirates who swiftly overwhelmed the sailors and stole everything on the ship. All the goods, all the personal treasures, even the clothes people were wearing. It was two days later when the ship limped into a foreign port.

The merchants knew no one in the city and had no money for food or to pay for a room.

The rabbi, however, went straight to the local synagogue and study house. There he was welcomed as a member of the faith. Once he began to teach, he was showered with gifts, good food and offers of hospitality.

The next day, the merchants were wandering sadly along the street when the rabbi passed them, well dressed, and surrounded by new friends.

'Now we see that your goods are of greater value than our gold, fine jewels and cloth,' the merchants said. 'We begin to realise that learning is the best form of goods.' "

A children's story

Introduction

● ●

> 'After all, economics should be simply about people getting together
> to set up local arrangements to provide the food and clothes
> and other things they need with a minimum of bother, so that
> they can then get on with what matters in life.'
> Ted Trainer, *Towards a Sustainable Economy*, 1996.

So YOU HAVE some money to invest. Perhaps you're in the fortunate position of earning more than you are spending. Perhaps you have received a legacy from the proverbial rich aunt, or inherited your parents' house. Whichever it is, you want to do something with the money apart from keeping it under the mattress.

There is no shortage of opportunity – indeed there is more money being earned from dealing in money than is earned from producing and distributing the goods and services we all need. According to the World Bank, there is ninety times as much money circulating in the world as there are goods and services to exchange. At the same time, ironically, many people the world over suffer an acute shortage of the money which they need to keep body and soul together.

Thus when you decide that your own small savings are going to enter this mad economic system, you face a heavy responsibility. A heavy responsibility to yourself to ensure you are satisfied with the way your money is used, the return it earns, the risk it takes, and any conditions attached to the investment contract you enter into. And also a heavy responsibility to others to ensure your money isn't being used to despoil the planet or exploit its peoples. This is particularly important because at present so much money is being invested in harmful activities, while many individuals and companies wishing to produce goods which genuinely contribute to human welfare find it extremely difficult to attract funds. Your money is sorely needed!

The most extraordinary aspect of ethical investment is that it exists as a concept at all. It would seem more normal to assume that *all* investment is ethical, while accepting there is a (very) tiny niche market for the exceptional *unethical* investment.

Ethical investment is growing by leaps and bounds within the UK and abroad, and while there is scepticism among some in the financial services industry about its viability, for increasing numbers of people it is financial and commonsense to consider ethics when investing money. In the UK, at least £1b is invested in the ethical unit trusts and related funds. In the US some $639b (nearly 9% of all investments) is invested with ethical considerations in mind.

This book attempts to explain in simple terms both the financial *and* ethical issues involved in investing money. It is unashamed in its approach that investors should consider ethical issues as important as financial ones. In this it takes a different stance from many in the ethical investment industry, particularly those running ethical unit trusts and similar plans, who believe that ethical investment is a 'niche market' on a par with Far Eastern stocks, or investments in particular forms of industrial companies.

I believe it is imperative that ethical criteria should play a central role in investment decisions. It is essential to show business people – who eventually receive the money through equities or loans – that we will not tolerate companies or governments which will destroy the earth or sell severely harmful products just so investors and directors can receive a few extra per cent. People's lives and dignity and the condition of the earth are worth far more.

If doing good is insufficient motivation for you to invest with Green standards in mind, an examination of the seriousness of the environmental dangers we all face should tip the balance. The damage we as consumers and businesses are doing to the earth, the air and the water are, many believe, sufficient to endanger the very life support systems which are crucial to our existence. If we don't invest ethically, *we may find we don't have pure water to drink, clean air to breathe, or healthy food to eat, let alone a good return on an investment.*

Most debate in the media about ethical investment has been about investments in the stockmarket and has revolved around whether such investments 'underperform' or 'outperform' the biggest and 'best' of public companies as expressed in the form of the various FT indexes. This is a blinkered approach. It implicitly assumes that ethical investors want the highest possible rate of return with ethics added-on. It also ignores the crying need from small companies, worker and housing co-operatives and 'social economy' undertakings for investment capital whose benefit to society can be far in excess of anything emanating from most publicly floated companies.

Consequently this book looks at the widest possible range of investments, of which those in companies listed on the stock market and their related funds are only one part. Inevitably it can be difficult to know where to draw the line – especially when looking at some of the investments now being promoted by charities believing in 'trade not aid'. We have included opportunities where the expectation is that the money invested can be recovered even if the return or profit may be negligible or non-existent, as well as the more usual investments where the aim is to achieve a good return. We also look at ways of spending money where such a move may be better than investing it: for example, the purchase of solar panels for water heating may be a better investment (in financial *and* environmental terms) than putting the same money into a long term investment account.

We also have deep concerns with the over-emphasis in the financial world on the highest monetary returns. The drawback of selling ethical investment based solely or mainly on the premise that it delivers above average profits, is that it follows that if returns dip, the investors will pull out and put their money back into companies which are seriously harming people and the planet. There *are* strong financial reasons for investing in ethical companies, but we believe the continual search for the very highest profits harms the socially useful companies which deliver more modest financial returns – but higher social and environmental benefits.

This approach is in marked contrast to that taken by most investment advisers, but we believe one of the drawbacks of the conventional investment world is that it does not take adequate account of issues outside the balance sheets.

Furthermore the world is full of people who made investments they later decided were 'unwise', and the tendency is to blame the financial interme-diary who described the opportunity as being full of promise of high returns and even 'as safe as houses'. Those watching the performance of the housing market know how hollow this expression now seems. All prospec-tuses carry the warning, 'You must remember that the performance of the investment may go down as well as up, and that past performance is no guide to how well the investment may perform in the future'.

This is a sentiment we heartily endorse, and we add: 'You must remember that the ethical standards of the investment may go down as well as up, and that past ethics are no guide to the standards to be adopted in the future'.

Prospectuses also advise potential investors to consult their independent financial adviser before making an investment. This we also endorse even though we have reservations about their knowledge of ethical issues. In the final analysis you who write out the cheques need to be absolutely sure you understand how the investment will operate: after that, your opinion of how the financial world will deliver the return is as good as anyone else's. The risk and responsibility are yours.

Throughout the book we have used the term 'ethical investment', though a number of other terms including 'Green investment', 'socially directed investment', and 'socially responsible investment' are also in use. All these latter terms, in our view, are variations on the same theme – which is the theme of this book – namely that the investor is considering *ethical* as well as financial issues when placing their money. Hence our decision to plump for the term ethical investment. Consideration of ethical factors, in our view, also leads investors to adopt Green criteria (protecting the planet and its peoples), as well as trying to make sure their investment is socially responsible, and directed to uses which have a social benefit.

Using the term, however, raises another difficult question: are investments which don't take into account ethics therefore unethical?. Well, many probably are, but not all of them by any means: the answer is rather to be found in the presumption that ethics should be an integral part of investing, and the highest ethical standards should be sought by all of us. If this book assists investors to raise those standards in their own savings and investments, then it will have succeeded.

This book could not have been written without the help of many both within and outside the financial services industry. While conducting interviews it became apparent very soon whether the individuals and companies concerned seriously want change in the economy so we live in balance with the planet, or whether offering ethical investments is simply another way to make money. Those committed to real change welcomed the idea of this book and made their offices, their time, and often even their files open to me. Those primarily interested in making money looked somewhat askance at a writer who had not emerged from the financial services industry itself daring to write such a book. This in itself sums up a major problem of the industry: all the investment opportunities written about here are on offer to ordinary people, and should be presented by the industry in such a way that ordinary people can easily understand how they operate. It should therefore not require special knowledge to write about them – nor to make the decisions on whether to invest.

Special thanks must go to Kate de Selincourt who proposed the idea; Lee Coates of the Ethical Investors Group for answering my many technical questions; Jon Carpenter, editor and publisher; Mark Campanale, Anne-Marie O'Connor, and Tessa Tennant of the National Provident Institution; Giles Chitty of Barchester Green Investment, Richard Tapper, Alex Macgillivray, Jane and David Straker, Michael Stimpson, Chris Mattingly, Paul Millsom, Anna Hywel-Davies, Val Oldaker, Craig McKenzie and my father Gerald Lang.

How investment money is used

● ●

U NDERSTANDING HOW MONEY is used is the first step in making a decision about how to invest it ethically. There are many intermediaries who will handle your investment before it reaches the people who use it for producing goods and services. The work of these intermediaries and the fees they receive are dealt with later. But eventually, after passing through many hands, (some of) your money will arrive in the accounts of those who need it.

There are four broad sectors where investment money is used: industry and commerce; governments; property and the financial world itself. Virtually every investment scheme will pass its money to one or more of these sectors, and the people working in these areas continually need your money to expand their work. The *financial* issue is whether this expansion will produce enough profit to pay you a return on your investment. The *ethical* issue is whether you want their particular work to expand or even continue at all.

There are two ways your money can be passed to these sectors: by being loaned to them or by them selling you a share in their business. If the money is a loan the recipient pays interest; if a share, they pay in the form of a dividend.

Money is needed by the four sectors in order to fund their work before it is earning income. Companies may sell shares to buy additional factories and modern machinery or to fund the research and development of new products. Building societies need money to lend to people wanting to buy their homes. The government may need cash for public projects which they believe will benefit the community. Companies expect to sell enough products and services in the future to allow them to pay their production costs; housebuyers expect future wages to provide the wherewithal to pay the mortgage; and governments expect there to be sufficient future tax income to pay back the bonds (see Chapter 6) which people buy.

In all cases those who use the money need to earn enough to pay back both the 'capital' originally borrowed, and the interest charged or profits paid out as dividends to shareholders.

Thus the higher the return demanded by investors, the higher the price of goods and services on sale. A business which has to pay 10% a year for its money over 25 years will pay back two and a half times the amount borrowed, and that money has to come from its earnings – in other words, its customers.

This system of lending money is essentially 'artificial'. That is, it has grown up in our economy without any serious consideration of what effect it has on the production of goods and services. In Muslim law, for example, it is forbidden to earn interest, and investors are supposed to take a share of the profits – or losses.

This mechanism which governs the use of money is not just of relevance to economists: it should be considered by all investors. If all those who invest in a group of food shops, for example, are willing to accept a lower return, they should be able to spend less on their weekly grocery bill as the company won't need to earn so much. One of Britain's most forward looking social banks, Triodos (see Chapter 8), takes this factor on board in their accounts. Depositors in some accounts at Triodos can choose the rate of interest they wish to receive (within a recommended range) and that rate determines how much is charged to borrowers.

The amount of return investors demand has important ramifications for making essential environmental changes. While some changes to protect the environment require people to consume less, or to be more efficient in the use of resources, many other changes demand investment in new infrastructure. The use of energy is one of the most pressing environmental issues (see Chapters 4 and 5) and most businesses pay for energy from sales income. If, however, a company wishes to reduce its energy use by investing in solar panels, wind generators, or combined heat and power plants, it generally funds such investment by borrowing money from a bank, or raising share capital. Thus the higher the return demanded by investors for providing this money, the less likely it is that the company will find it economic to introduce the environmentally beneficial changes. This is because the cost of borrowing the money has to be compared with the income from sales which comes to them interest free and is used to pay the quarterly energy bills.

Many environmental improvements could thus become financially viable if money was available at low interest rates. Similar issues apply when companies are considering changing their operations. A company considering moving out of defence into peaceful production may be discouraged by the cost of obtaining money to fund the changes.

While economic activity and the profit a company makes provide for the payment of returns on investments, a further factor comes into play for those putting money into the stock market. The gain to be had from shares in companies comes firstly in terms of dividends – these are simply a share of the profits distributed to all shareholders. But investors also expect to gain their money on shares through a second route – that is a rise in the value of the shares themselves as they are traded on the Stock Exchange. This rise is theoretically based on how well the company (and the economy) is doing. As more people try to buy the shares of a particular company, the price of the shares rise, and anyone selling them takes more profit. Most of the activity on the Stock Exchange is carried out as dealers, large institutions, and wealthy individuals buy and sell shares based on their personal predictions as to whether the price is to go up or down. All are aiming to buy shares when they are cheap, and sell them when they are high. Such activity plays little part in producing the goods and services people need – as when there is a stock market slump, people 'lose' vast sums of money, yet the underlying companies, managers, workers, skills and plant are still in place and able to produce. These rises and falls in publicly quoted companies are one of the reasons why small businesses not listed on the Stock Exchange find it diffi-cult to attract investment since they cannot produce the profits from this continual reselling of shares.

All investments therefore rest on a fundamental presumption: that the economy will continue to expand and businesses will become larger and produce bigger profits. While this presumption is barely questioned in the financial world, many people believe the economy cannot continue growing indefinitely because the planet won't allow it to. The industrial nations aim at an expansion rate of about three per cent a year, which would result in a doubling of industrial production every 25 years.

It is at this point that those who doubt the worth of ethical investment need to focus their minds. The workings of the planet have already caused some industries to cease expanding: asbestosis killed the asbestos industry, huge claims for the clean up of contaminated land (particularly in the US) is causing severe problems to the insurance industry, and the destruction of the ozone layer is killing the production of CFCs. Future victims could include the motor industry as governments start restricting car use because of rising asthma levels in cities and global warming caused by vehicle exhaust fumes; and the chemical industry could lose its profits from nitrate or chlo-rine production as we become faced with ever more polluted underground water courses.

Thus ethical investment is not just a matter of conscience: it is the logical conclusion of an informed and rigorous assessment of the likely returns from different forms of investment.

2

Preliminary considerations

●●●

'...The noisy clutter of life in England where nowadays it seems there is too much prosperity for real happiness and too much hurry for humour.'
Lillian Beckwith, *The Sea for Breakfast*, 1961.

THERE ARE SEVERAL major factors to consider when deciding where to place your money. The interplay of these factors will influence how the money can be used, what it can earn and how it can be an influence for good in the world. Investors can predict how some of these factors will operate over a period of time, but many may operate entirely unexpectedly. All of them will change as the months and years pass, and none can be counted on, as even the most secure and apparently stable investment can suddenly undergo extreme changes in the fast changing financial world.

The principal factors to consider when making an ethical investment are:

The financial risk involved

In the world of high (and low) finance, the greater the risk of losing the money, the higher the return demanded; and conversely, the lower the risk, the lower the return.

Thus if you place money in a building society, you are virtually certain to be paid the advertised interest, and be able to obtain your money back when you want it. Consequently the rate of interest payable is comparatively low – a few per cent per year. The risk to the money is in the unlikely event that a building society becomes insolvent. This is possible, but tight regulations govern such societies and so the chance is very low. Situations where it could happen would be if a society was being run criminally – that is, the directors had stolen sizeable sums of money – or if the housing market experienced a major crash and huge numbers of borrowers (far more than are affected by the 'negative equity' trap of the mid nineties) defaulted on their payments. Even if a building society were to crash, the industry has a compensation scheme which would go some way to making up losses.

A high risk investment is likely to involve putting money into an entirely new business, perhaps being set up by a person with a seemingly good idea but little business experience. 'Venture capital' investors putting money into such businesses would expect a return as high as 30 per cent a year. But in the view of most conventional financiers and banks, such new businesses have a very high chance of not selling enough of their product and consequently going bust, with the result that investors could lose virtually all the money they've put in. Even if the company is profitable it will still be seen as high risk because, as it won't be a public company, there is less likely to be a ready market if an investor wants to sell their shares at any time.

It is important to remember that when the financial world talk about 'risk' they are only talking about the *financial* risk to the investor. They are not talking about any ethical or environmental risks, nor are they talking about financial risks to other stakeholders such as employees. So the fact that a company making nitrates could be causing the pollution of water supplies is not a 'risk' in the eyes of a financial adviser unless it seems that the company is going to be sued for the damage or prohibited from marketing the chemical to farmers. Similarly 'risk' isn't a factor if money is being raised by a company to allow it to purchase new machinery which would cause redundancies and therefore financial risk to those losing their jobs.

The length of time the money is to be invested

Generally, investors receive better rates if they are prepared to pledge their money for a long period or are prepared to invest fixed amounts at specified intervals. This is because the money is more useful if the recipient knows how long it will be before it is demanded back. Knowing when it has to be paid back means a business can, for example, plan its production and cash flow so that it has cash to repay the sum when it is needed. If they need to be constantly on guard because the money could be demanded back at any time, they have to plan accordingly, and that could mean keeping other assets more 'liquid', that is more easily saleable should they need to raise cash quickly. It also costs less in administration charges if the money is pledged for a longer period of time.

Whether the money is loaned or used to buy shares

Money provided on loan involves a comparatively simple arrangement: a contract is entered into which requires the borrower to pay back the sum on demand, over a period of time, or on a fixed date, with interest payable on top. Money deposited with banks or building societies is 'lent' by the investor. The relationship between the borrower and the lender is usually a distant one: the lender/investor generally has limited rights (and often limited interest) in influencing how the money is used on a day to day basis.

Money used to buy shares, however, means the person providing the money receives a share in the company in return. This share entitles the investor to a proportion of the profits that the company makes and also allows them to attend the company's annual general meetings and (theoretically) influence the working of the company and nominate and elect the directors. In the world of huge public companies this part-ownership is more apparent than real, but directors do feel they need to listen to their small shareholders.

The investor can make money not only by receiving a share of the profits in the form of dividends, but also by selling the shares on at a profit to other potential investors. This is the main business of the Stock Exchange as shares are bought and sold each day, with the volume of sales influencing the price, and therefore the profits or losses shareholders are making. There is little difference in the financial risk involved between making a loan to a company and buying shares in it: if a company goes to the wall, individuals who have loaned it money or bought shares are likely to be equally at risk (though those granting loans do come somewhat higher up the list of creditors than share-holders, and there are special conditions for the owners of particular types of bonds – see Chapter 6). The risk generally is according to the *type of organ-isation* the money is given to: money put into a company is generally at greater risk than that put into a bank or building society, which in turn are not as safe as government bonds, which are loans to the government – the conventional wisdom being that governments don't go bust.

Whether to invest through the Stock Exchange

Investment opportunities can be divided into those involving public compa-nies quoted on the Stock Exchange and the financial contracts linked to them; and those involving companies and institutions not quoted. You can invest directly into public companies, or via arrangements such as unit trusts or pension plans. These investments may be less risky than investing in non-quoted companies, though not necessarily less risky than investing in a building society or bank. Publicly quoted companies are generally regulated more tightly than non-public companies, but they are also much bigger. Thus it is more difficult to assess whether they will meet your ethical criteria, and when there is mismanagement or worse, the effect is greater.

Screening out investments

The easiest approach for ethical investors to take is to simply refuse to put money into particular sectors or particular companies. This can be done by ensuring that no money goes, for example, into companies which manufac-ture armaments, or tobacco products, or which have a low number of women in senior positions. The investor can choose the criteria, and there are screening services which examine companies so some sort of informed deci-sion can be made about whether to invest in one company or another, or one unit trust or another.

Investors need to be sure in their own minds where to draw the line. A decision to refuse to invest in tobacco companies could also exclude supermarkets which sell tobacco. Or a decision not to invest in companies which supply to the armed forces could encompass a food company which supplied potatoes to the army. Most of the debate within the ethical investment world has centred around how ethical is ethical, and with the complex interconnected world of high finance today, an arch critic will find something to be concerned about in virtually all investments in public companies and large banks. This is not to say you're on a hiding to nothing for even trying, but it's important to be aware that if you're going to rely just on screening out companies and banks, you'll need to make some hard decisions.

Furthermore, if all you are doing is not investing in bad companies or banks, the influence you are having can be limited if these companies are not told forcefully and regularly that people are refusing to invest in them because they are dissatisfied with their ethical or Green performance. After all, people refrain from investing for a variety of reasons, and unless the companies are told why, they may just think you're chasing better returns elsewhere and so they'd better attempt to sell more of their unacceptable product to attract your money back!

Actively seeking out highly ethical investments

This approach takes ethical investors right to the heart of ensuring that money is used constructively and that business and banking that contribute to human and environmental welfare receive the input they need.

Some financial specialists believe that only by operating ruthlessly in the market can a business flourish and the investor receive good returns. As a result many socially useful projects find it very difficult to obtain the funding they need. At the most basic level, a poor family finds it next to impossible to borrow money to pay to insulate their home or install solar panels. Yet these would produce good rates of financial return, as well as being essential if we are to reduce our CO_2 outputs and use of nuclear power and coal. A small business without adequate security will find it similarly difficult to obtain finance for such investments. The investor who actively seeks out beneficial ways of using their money will be providing a far greater social good than those who simply screen out some of the companies listed on the Stock Exchange.

The involvement you want in your investments

Some investments give the investor no opportunity for involvement in deciding where their money is lodged, while others positively encourage shareholder or lender activity. Putting your money in a conventional high street bank gives you virtually no say in how your money is used and since banks will maintain the confidentiality of their customers, it is very likely you won't even know to whom or for what it is subsequently being lent. Investments in unit trusts will allow you to know where the money is being invested, but won't allow you to attend the companies' annual general meetings where at least you can ask questions about their financial and ethical performance. Investing in the social economy, however, may give you the opportunity to meet at first hand the people who will use the money and possibly to participate in their work.

Whether to seek out unethical companies

Since shareholders are the only group who have the right to formally meet and question company directors (see Chapter 11) it is worth considering buying some shares in companies in order to influence them to adopt ethical standards. If you have difficulties accepting any profits which may come your way, you could give the money to a worthy cause, or use it to publicise your success at influencing the company.

Two further issues are also very important. The first is that in the world of money, it is very rare that anything is static. A company which today has no women on the board may appoint three tomorrow. A company which is producing an environmentally damaging chemical today may cease production tomorrow. A unit trust fund which has a good record of choosing profitable investments may suddenly start performing badly because their accomplished fund manager has retired. An interest rate from the bank may have seemed low compared to another investment last week, but this week the bank rate may go up, and so their accounts become more attractive. While some investors delight in the daily cut and thrust of the financial markets, most view (or should view) money as a means to an end, and as a way to protect savings for a rainy day and do some good in the world.

Second, the bottom line is that all investments are reliant on how the economy, people, and the environment are going to perform in the future. *No one, but no one* is able to predict exactly what is going to happen, so when you're examining details of a financial opportunity, bear in mind that the company selling it is unable to give you the one piece of information you need to make up your mind: exactly how your investment will perform, and how well it will be used.

Indeed investments are the only 'service' we buy where the seller won't tell us what we're getting for our money – in marked contrast to the information available to help us make our mind up when we buy all the other items we spend money on such as food, clothing, furniture, heating systems, houses, cars and even luxuries.

Selling bad investments

When you begin to invest ethically you have to face the question of how to deal with unacceptable investments you already hold.

The question throws up a paradox: you are likely to want a good return on your investment and that may mean wanting the price to rise. For that to happen the companies providing the basis for the investment need to sell more of their unacceptable products in their unacceptable way so they return higher profits, a greater dividend, a higher share price, and thus a rise in the unit trust price or greater ability to pay interest on a bond.

So, because you hold the investment, you are almost forced to wish for the profits you don't really want to make.

The position is exacerbated by the pricing formula for many investments. Shares and unit trusts operate using two prices: the price they are sold to the public being higher than the rate they are bought back for. The difference constitutes the overheads and profits for the dealers. Long term plans such as pensions and life assurance often impose severe penalties for cashing them in before the contract has ended. People paying into a pension plan may receive far less than they have paid in if they try to back out within the first few years.

Unfortunately there is no alternative to taking the bit between your teeth: you may need to decide between selling and making a profit from a trade you disapprove of, or selling and making a loss.

There are, however, a few peripheral issues it is worth considering:

(1) Some companies will buy back their shares from investors. They do so because they are in less need of the money, and want instead to reduce the spread of ownership. Thus selling your shares back to the company has the effect of taking cash from them, so they have less to spend on investing in trading you disapprove of.

(2) Consider retaining a few shares to use to pressurise the company to improve its operations. The ownership of even one share gives you the right to attend the company's AGM and put your views to the directors (see Chapter 11).

(3) Some pressure groups want shares so their supporters can attend AGMs, so consider donating a few shares to groups such as the World Development Movement, Friends of the Earth, Baby Milk Action or Greenpeace. There is no central clearing house for people wanting to donate shares in this manner, but Lee Coates of the Ethical Investors Group will keep a record of shares which investors are prepared to make available to pressure groups.

(4) When you are selling, make sure you write to the company or institution telling them it is their poor ethical or green standards which are causing you to disinvest.

3

How your money reaches your investments

• •

'The plan was to start off with the largest possible capitalisation
and then sell all the stock and all the bonds that could be sold.
Whatever money happened to be left over after all the stock and
bond-selling expenses and promoters' charges and all that, went
grudgingly into the foundation of the business. A good business was
not one that did good work and earned a fair profit. A good business
was one that would give the opportunity for the floating of a large
amount of stocks and bonds at high prices.'

Henry Ford, *My Life and Work.*

YOUR MONEY WILL generally pass through several pairs of hands before
it reaches the people who will actually use it.

These financial intermediaries provide advice, set up financial contracts
which govern how your money is used, and carry out the buying and selling
of the various contracts.

In general the more complicated the financial arrangement, the more
intermediaries there will be. Money invested in a pension scheme, for
instance, may pass from your bank where you have an account, to a financial adviser, to the pension company which will buy from a unit trust
company which buys company shares through a stockbroker. When you
retire the stockbroker will sell the shares and the unit trust will pass a lump
sum of money to the pension company which will purchase an annuity from
another company which will pay your pension from their bank account. You
will then pay the cheque into your own bank account, and it's available for
you to spend.

These individuals and companies constitute the financial services industry
and they receive their income by taking a percentage of the money passing
through their hands, or by a set fee per transaction.

Because the return on money is not a 'product' which can be handled,
eaten, tried or tested, those working in the financial services industry have

adopted a particular approach to how they present themselves. While most products can be bought from a range of different types of outlet – large and small clothes shops, different types of food outlets, car sales rooms with potted plants or on semi-derelict lots on back streets – financial services are sold by people with almost identical presentation.

The image of mature men (most are men) in discreet suits working from quiet offices with smart secretaries is intended to convey solidity, sobriety, probity, knowledge, and financial acumen. There is no reason why such an appearance should imply great knowledge of the financial markets, but that is the almost universal standard. But it should be remembered that all this is artificial and different standards could be adopted. In Bangladesh, for instance, the Grameen Bank has become very successful by lending small amounts of money to (mainly) women using the technique of roving bank 'managers' who travel the country on bicycles with satchels of money.

The literature produced by the financial industry also has a particular image and focuses on the reputation of the provider, with liberal smatterings of technical terms, but often a staggering absence of hard facts. Some financial plans are described as 'exciting' but quite how the excitement is to be gained is unclear. Nearly all concentrate on financial returns expressed in vague phrases such as 'solid rates of return' and 'an above average opportunity'. One company describes itself as 'highly respected in the UK insurance and investment industry, recognised for a comprehensive range of products, competitively priced products, quality service, and a record for producing consistent returns for its customers'. Another offers an 'option that will, because of its sheer flexibility and refreshing lack of restrictions, provide you with the incentive to give yourself the retirement you so richly deserve'. A critical observer might conclude that 'consistent returns' may mean consistently low returns; while 'flexibility and lack of restrictions' may allow managers to invest where they like, but the essential issue is whether the fund manager invests wisely.

Another fund says it aims to 'maximise long term capital and income growth', presumably the aim of most, if not all, investors. This fund's annual report for the year ending February 1995 revealed that their income units fell 12.4% over the year, compared to which the FT-SE All Share Index (which is a measure of the average rise or fall of Stock Exchange companies) fell by 11.2%. Nevertheless, the report continues, 'good growth in the UK economy seems set to continue', and 'the prospects for the — Fund seem encouraging'.

Prospectuses for ethical investments will give some explanation of the ethical standards applied, but apart from these there is often a paucity of information about how the money is actually to be used. Indeed many investments say nothing whatever about what the funds are actually wanted for.

Since January 1995 financial intermediaries have had to declare how much they are to receive in terms of fees, and many potential customers have been shocked to learn that with schemes such as pensions, as much as a third of what they pay in may go as payments to the companies which set up the plans (see Chapter 7). But while the fees need to be declared, most investors have little alternative but to trust the regulatory bodies and the honesty of the people they deal with.

It is extremely difficult to compare the fees with other options before you invest your money, and even more difficult to ascertain whether the correct fees have been deducted – particularly with plans such as pensions and bonds where money is invested for long periods. In addition, if the investor does become dissatisfied with the fees being charged, it is often difficult to extricate oneself from investments as there are usually penalties for early withdrawals.

While even the ethical sector has its shortcomings in this area, prospective investors dealing with a company for whom ethical investment is their *raison d'être* may feel more secure than one whose sole reason for existence is to make money. The latter tend to look askance at those few financial advisers who all but campaign to persuade investors to adopt ethical standards, but people who trade among, for instance green businesses, will know there is a lower chance of them meeting blatant dishonesty than in the conventional business world. But while you may choose an adviser on the grounds of their ethical preferences, it does not necessarily mean you have chosen an adviser who is better at his or her job.

4

The ethical issues

••

'Doing right solely for reasons of profit leads to a cessation of so doing, with a return to bad old ways when profit fails. Far better to do right for the right reasons. If I save a woman from drowning because she owes me money, or because I seek her affection, I act from self-interest, not ethics. Woe betide the woman if she neither debtor nor desired be'.
Peter Cave, letter to *The Guardian*, 1995.

THE EXPRESSION 'one person's meat is another's poison' could have been coined with ethical investment in mind. Conventional investors have it easy: they only have to look at a (publicly quoted) company's 'bottom line', decide whether the management know what they're about and whether customers are likely to buy, pop their cheque in the post and await the profits or losses. But ethical investors are likely to be well aware that there are many activities being carried out by companies and governments seeking their money which cause great harm to the world we live in.

Investors can get little or no help from financial advisers about which ethical issues should be considered. Good ethical advisers should be able to say which companies are involved in particularly undesirable activities, but they draw back from doing anything to persuade you to adopt a particular standard. They believe they exist to give *financial* advice, not to campaign. This contrasts with the pressure groups, which have organised high profile campaigns to persuade investors to remove their funds from particular industries and banks. One principal target has been the high street banks which the World Development Movement, among others, has suggested should be boycotted because of their lending and interest-charging policies to Third World countries. The governments of some of these countries now owe so much money to these banks that annual interest payments alone (due in 'hard' currency) can be more than the total value of their exports or even their gross national product.

The issues to be considered are wide and various and investors will soon realise it is not simply a question of deciding to exclude an activity they view as damaging. The work of a modern company is complex and far-reaching, and it is likely to have fingers in many pies. So an objection, say, to using products tested on animals may seem a simple issue. But do you refuse to invest in a group of shops, which sells thousands of products, of which one uses an ingredient tested on animals many years ago by another company?

Furthermore, the products sold and the manufacturing methods employed should be only two of an investor's concerns. Others may include how the workforce is treated; whether there is a reasonable proportion of women, people from ethnic minority groups, or those with disabilities in senior positions; how the company responds to complaints; whether it is registered in tax havens; how large it is; how it advertises; whether it gives money to charity – or an undesirable political party; and how it treats trade unions.

Nor is there necessarily any final agreement on what is ethical and what is not as individual investors can take contrasting views on an issue. A person concerned about steeply climbing population growth may want to invest in companies producing contraceptives. Conversely, an investor belonging to a religion which bans contraception may want to specifically exclude such investments. Similarly where two countries are at war, some investors might want to invest in companies operating on one side and not the other, while other investors may have entirely the opposite loyalties.

Environmental and social auditing

It has been many years since companies were first required to produce regular financial reports which are independently audited. The reports are produced so that those running the company, the investors and regulators can see, in a standard form, its financial state of health.

The 1990s have spawned two further areas of company reporting. Environmental audits are now being commissioned by many large companies to examine their impact on the environment and how it can be minimised. While the practitioners of environmental auditing have formed professional associations to set standards, for most audits there are as yet no legislative requirements to meet.

Social audits are at an even earlier stage of development. This is a technique developed by the New Economics Foundation whereby a company examines its impact on its stakeholders: the workforce, customers, suppliers, local community, and trade unions.

In the mid 1990s only a handful of companies had commissioned environmental and social audits, and naturally it is the more socially responsible companies which have. Ethical investors seeking information about companies should ask whether such reports have been produced – and imply that investments won't be considered unless they have and show a willingness by the company to take ethical issues seriously.

You may feel it is better to use your money to encourage good practice. So if a firm announces it is to change one part of its work to make it more ethical, it might be wise to invest some money with them – with the intention of stating that a bigger investment will be made if the company improves its record even further.

Excluding companies because of their undesirable activities may not be the most constructive way of making sure your money is used well. A better practice is to actively seek out companies doing socially useful work – and this is likely to take you out of the stock market altogether and into the world of small businesses, worker and housing co-operatives, housing associations, and the social economy where charity and business move ever closer together.

In this chapter we look at a range of ethical issues. The list is not exclusive, and inevitably concerns are left out for reasons of space. You may feel the best way to regard the list is as a restaurant menu: you are not expected to eat every dish!

I have included *my* principal concerns when looking at each of these issues: inevitably *your* priorities may be different and it is, of course, for you to weigh up each of the issues to decide which you judge to be more important when investing your money. Such judgements will also lead you to include many factors not addressed here, and dismiss some that are important to me.

The arguments for excluding investment in any of these practices have chiefly to do with whether dangers are 'proven', and whether your resulting list of exclusions means there is an adequate selection of places left to put your money.

ADVERTISING

Advertising is one of Britain's largest industries. Companies plead they need to advertise in order to achieve 'volume sales' which allow them to keep prices low. In actual practice 15% or more of the price paid for most goods goes to pay for the advertising – and a dose of healthy scepticism towards the whole advertising industry will stand customer and investor in good stead.

More insidiously the sheer barrage of advertising seen by most people can lead to a mistaken awareness that the only way to happiness is to buy the various products on sale. There is little counterbalancing advertising suggesting that happiness and contentment in life come in many different guises, such as having a wide circle of friends, being close to your family, enjoying many free occupations such as walking or cycling or chatting with neighbours. Such routes to happiness are not advertised because no one can earn money from selling them. Advertising for products also has a sting in the tail: buying the product can't be allowed to make you too happy as the company will want you to buy something else next week.

Thus how a company advertises should be of interest to an investor: many advertisements make unjustified claims about products, or insidiously aim at children or exploit people's fears. Advertising agencies can work for companies and organisations doing useful work, as well as businesses which are positively harmful. The power of advertising should not be underestimated, even though many people would claim not to be influenced by it.

ALCOHOL

The marketing of alcoholic liquor was one of the earliest targets for ethical investors, and indeed for social reformers. While it is generally agreed that alcohol in moderation is harmless (and some doctors even believe that drinking in moderation contributes to good health), the effects of excess alcohol are tragic to see.

Recent evidence suggests that chemical additives in some drinks are a greater contributor to aggression than the alcohol itself. This is an additional argument for investing in small local breweries and wineries using organic ingredients.

ANIMALS

Many industries regard animals as simply another product in the industrial equation and treat them accordingly.

Animals are used for experiments and producing food. The former rightly arouses most ire, particularly because many creatures are put through unspeakable horrors to test the effectiveness and safety of items such as cosmetics which, while desired by some, are hardly an essential perquisite of life and can be tested in other ways. Many ethical unit trust funds will bar investment in companies using animals for such research, but will not exclude companies using animals for genuinely medical experiments. The latter is a more difficult area, with some scientists stating that the results gained from tests on animals are of limited use when applied to humans. Nevertheless many people will accept experimentation for medical purposes only, and not for other reasons.

The number of people who don't eat meat is steadily growing in the UK for a number of reasons. Many people are appalled by the methods of modern livestock production, in particular the adding of chemicals such as growth promoters to animal feedstuff, and intensive production where chickens, pigs, and calves spend their lives crammed into unlit sheds. Furthermore, in a world where many people do not get enough to eat, there is concern that far more land is needed to produce meat than other crops.

BIOTECHNOLOGY

The new science of biotechnology involves artificial manipulation of DNA, the 'genetic code of life'. The science spans agriculture, pharmaceuticals and heavy industry. Changes to living creatures and crops have aroused the most concern. Tomatoes have been genetically altered so they have a firmer skin, while oil seed rape varieties have been engineered to be immune to weed-killers. The latter example provides an illustration of the dangers, for oil seed rape is a weed as well as a crop and plants spread outside the fields where they are sown. Naturalists fear we are storing up a severe ecological danger for the future. Seeds too have been genetically altered, and then their availability restricted through patenting, a move which has justifiably provoked outrage in countries such as India where seed varieties which formed the basis of genetic research were developed by poor peasant farmers.

BIRTH CONTROL

This only involves a very small number of companies. The arguments for investing reflect concerns about the steeply rising population and the material poverty which can result from trying to keep large numbers of children on a small income. The rise in the world population is causing humans to occupy more land than ever before, and to consume more and more resources. If population continues to grow at its present pace, we could all be facing severe scarcities while the planet will become increasingly unable to support us. This is not to ignore the fact that people in the industrialised world are consuming far more resources per head than those in the Third World – it is simply that the planet cannot support an ever growing population.

The pressures against investing in companies involved in birth control are principally religious, with some groups such as the Roman Catholics believing that birth control in any form is 'sinful'.

There are also deep concerns about the ethical practices adopted by some companies when they provide contraceptives to poor people in the Third World. These include accusations that inadequate explanations are given and that some contraceptives deemed unsafe in the West are nevertheless aggressively marketed in the Third World.

CULTURAL UNIFORMITY

As companies have spread their trading right across the world, so they are spreading a monoculture where people are just seen as markets. Thus high streets in Asia, Africa, America and Europe are starting to feature the same shops fitted out in the same way, serving identical products. The world of fast food is the worst culprit, and the identical shops and cafés are slowly eating away at individual cultures.

Some countries, such as France and India, have tried to resist such encroachments, but many nations, particularly in the Third World, want the investment and believe that well-known Western companies add cachet to their high streets.

In addition to a denuding of culture and individuality, the internationalisation of trade makes it increasingly difficult for small local businesses to flourish.

If you have any doubts about the bad effects of cultural uniformity, a visit to a few high streets in the UK will reveal broadly similar shops selling broadly similar goods: townscapes which are depressingly uniform across the country.

ENVIRONMENTAL ISSUES

Concern for the environment relates to the use of energy and resources, and pollution. The arguments for including environmental concerns is a simple one: the world we live on is finite, and if we damage its life support systems, humans as a species could be seriously affected, and other species of both plant and animal could die out. The Western industrialised nations have been built on the principle of using many finite raw materials with little thought of what will happen when they run out, and dumping waste without recognising that we may be doing irrevocable harm in the process.

My view is that if people don't plan to change to a sustainable economy, the planet will force us to. Hence as a particular environmental issue becomes more pressing, it will become ever more difficult to continue as we did before. So, for example, the adding of lead to petrol caused brain damage, particularly to children, and as a consequence many motorists have switched to unleaded fuel following the introduction of a tax advantage. However lead has other environmental problems, so investment in companies producing lead is inadvisable for ethical, environmental and financial reasons.

Energy production. Companies involved in producing or distributing energy from finite sources such as coal, gas and oil should be treated cautiously: future generations may not thank us for squandering these materials. Coal burning for electricity results in the emission of a cocktail of gases which are major contributors to global warming – the heating of the earth's atmosphere – and acid rain which is causing severe damage to trees. Burning gas causes less damage, but much is wasted. Nuclear energy does not come from a finite source but the ever increasing amount of radioactive waste will need to be stored for thousands of years – periods of time outside the experience of all of us and especially the business people running the stations. In addition, the effects of accidents in nuclear facilities are horrifying, and despite the protestations of the UK nuclear industry Chernobyl, Three Mile Island and Sellafield illustrate that accidents can happen anywhere.

Investments in companies operating sustainable energy sources would be a better use of money.

Resource use. Environmentalists divide the earth's resources into those which are finite and those which replenish themselves. Finite resources are those which cannot be replaced once they have been used up: e.g. minerals, oil, gas and coal. Replenishable resources are those that nature naturally replenishes or produces such as the wind and sun, trees and crops. Predictions of how long particular finite resources will last play down the fact that they will become increasingly scarce and expensive as it becomes more costly to extract them, and that at some time the reserves will be exhausted.

Investors who care for the environment (or who have children!) should therefore avoid companies whose work is reliant on extensive use of finite resources, and especially those which squander these resources. Conversely, investments in businesses which use sustainable resources such as organic agriculture, mixed forestry, and renewable energy are deserving of support.

Pollution. Industry is pouring out pollutants into the water, air, and soil, and many of them are accumulating in quantities which are damaging wildlife and humans. We are all aware of rivers in industrialised cities which have few fish and are unsafe for swimming. Such pollution is reaching the sea from the discharge of chemicals, sewage and nuclear waste. The soil is suffering from the contents of industrial and domestic waste dumped in land-fill sites; and air quality is affected by discharges from factory chimneys, vehicle exhausts, and power stations.

There are already signs that this pollution is causing serious harm: the output of CFCs from aerosols and refrigerators has led to a thinning of the ozone layer which in turn is leading to increases in some forms of cancer. Emissions of CO_2 from factories, vehicles and power stations is expected to lead to a rise in global temperatures which will cause upheavals in agriculture and possibly a melting of the ice caps with a resultant rise in sea levels.

Run-off of nitrates applied to non-organic farms is believed to be seeping into watercourses and entering drinking water; while evidence is coming forward to indicate that electromagnetic radiation from power lines is contributing to an increase in cancers.

Regulations limiting pollution and the punishments for transgressing companies are believed by many environmentalists to be too lax, and investors should avoid companies which are not taking these issues seriously.

Tropical rainforests. Evidence suggests that a large proportion of the world's species are to be found in the rich web of life in these forests – yet we know comparatively little about them. We do, however, know that many of the tribespeople living there are losing their homes and culture as the trees are cleared. We also know these tribes have knowledge of the medicinal qualities of certain plants of which we are profoundly ignorant. Furthermore the rainforests act as a CO_2 'store' and cutting them down can increase the rate of global warming.

Forests are facing severe depredations from large companies keen to exploit the timber and to use the land which subsequently becomes available. It is not an understatement to say that the rainforests are vital to the planet's and our survival and I would recommend investors to avoid companies suspected of operating in them unless it is absolutely clear they are not damaging them.

Profit or loss?

Mainstream investors will often object to introducing ethics to investment decisions because they claim it will reduce the profits investors make.

There is by no means overwhelming support for this view, and a report by the Royal Society for the Encouragement of Arts, Manufactures and Commerce indicates the opposite may be the case. The RSA took two years to compile their report which examined the long term records of large companies. They conclude that 'an over-reliance on purely financial measures stops many companies making the top grade and staying there'. They cite the example of the 11 companies which topped a profitability survey between 1979 and 1989. Since then two of them have been bought out, and four collapsed. The report says 'companies which rely solely on financial measures of success are exposing shareholders to unnecessary risks'.

The RSA suggest companies should focus less on financial measures of success.

While this may be a minority view among conventional investors, there is greater support for believing that taking environmental issues into account may mean greater profits, not less.

The reason is simply that environmental degradation is fast catching up with us, and will cost a lot of money to put right. Companies which have been unfortunate enough to operate in environmentally unsound sectors are finding to their cost that changing their operations and cleaning up pollution can adversely affect their profits. It is now almost routine that an accident at an industrial plant will cause the owning company's shares to dip steeply. In the United States industrial giants are locked into court battles with their insurers over who will pay out for cleaning up the thousands of sites contaminated with dangerous chemicals. In the UK, the makers of asbestos suffered severe losses as a result of litigation.

In 1994 the investment managers of pension funds and insurance companies received one of the UK's first 'alternative prospectuses' when the company European Vinyls Corporation offered 9m shares for sale. EVC's own official prospectus stated 'The fundamentals for PVC are beginning to show dramatic improvement ... as construction activity continues to grow in Europe, the US, and the Far East'.

Greenpeace however, stated: 'Environmental and safety pressures, led by concerns over dioxins and other toxic emissions arising during accidental fires, will begin to impact on PVC demand in construction applications. Regulatory and market pressures associated with dioxins and other organochlorines, the most serious pollutants associated with PVC production, use and disposal, will intensify in the light of very recent developments in the US which threaten to apply pressures in markets that have so far remained relatively unaffected, such as the UK, France, Spain and Italy. A valuation of EVC made on the basis of [the official prospectus] would, in our view, overstate the company's worth'.

In other words, don't buy these shares if you want to make a profit.

EVC, as would be expected, denied these accusations, but the relevant issue is that in this case green concerns coincide exactly with anxiety over whether the investment will be profitable.

EVC is but one company, but environmental concerns can affect profits of an entire industrial sector. Delphi International Ltd. is a financial advisory firm 'that helps clients to benefit from the investment opportunities arising out of the shift to more environmentally-sustainable development'. In 1994 they produced a report on the investment potential of the carbon-fuel industry in the light of global warming and climate change.

They summarise the position: 'Climate change presents one of the most serious global environmental challenges humanity has ever faced. The implications could affect a great variety of businesses directly and indirectly, and will have increasing relevance in determining the investment prospects and financial risks for a wide variety of companies... Climate change presents long term major risks to the carbon-fuel industry. The risks have not yet been adequately discounted by the financial markets. Investors should therefore avoid maintaining long term overweight positions in the carbon-fuel industry until such effects are adequately discounted'. Delphi suggest instead that investors should look at the 'alternative energy industry (which) offers greater growth prospects ... diversification into this sector also offers substantial scope to offset the risks of climate change effectively'. Lest investors dismiss such prophecies as doom-laden claims without substance, the report quotes British Gas as admitting that 'the production and use of oil and gas cannot be regarded as behaving sustainably'.

While there is an emerging scientific consensus on the dangers of global warming, knowledge of the effects of electromagnetic radiation has received less attention. Such radiation is emitted from electric cables and there is some evidence to suggest it causes cancer. There are a number of court actions pending in both the UK and the US seeking damages for illnesses alleged to be caused by power lines – both above and below ground.

Such actions (two of which have been successful) are causing insurance companies to exclude such claims from their policies granted to electricity companies. If electromagnetic radiation is proved in the courts to cause cancer, the financial repercussions on electricity and insurance companies are likely to be immense, with a consequent dip in share values. If the electricity utilities need to raise their prices to the consumer to pay for such costs, the knock-on effect on industry will also be considerable.

RESPONSIVENESS

Some companies are a law unto themselves: they set out on a course of action, and won't change it come hell or high water. They operate as though the views of people around them are of no concern. Thus investors should consider how well a company responds to public pressure.

Exxon Oil gained far greater public notoriety after the oil spill in Alaska because it steadfastly resisted pressures to provide adequate funding for the clean up. Its public reputation probably suffered far more from this obstinate attitude than from the spillage itself.

In my view companies should realise they are part of the wider community, and investors should be reluctant to put their money into unheeding companies and should not automatically believe them when they say they've changed.

GAMBLING

The practice of putting down a small stake and hoping to win a large prize has been catapulted into public attention following the introduction of the National Lottery.

Gambling can become a disease, with victims wagering more and more money in the mistaken belief that the next press of the button, the run of the horse or the number generated by a computer will be the 'big one' and that when it happens it will bring them instant happiness.

The National Lottery itself was sold to the public on the basis that it would raise money for charities and other good causes. In practice only a very small proportion of the price of each lottery ticket goes to such causes (most of the income funds the prizes and goes to the government in tax). In addition, early allocations by the operating company raised eyebrows as the targets did not appear to be 'good causes' in the way the bulk of the public understand them. There's also evidence that charitable donations dropped considerably during the first months of the lottery's operation.

In the slightly less salubrious world of high street amusement arcades, there is evidence of addiction by schoolchildren to the machines; while in the public mind casinos often seem to appeal to those tied up with serious crime.

Finally, some readers might feel that if you object to gambling, you shouldn't be making investments at all, since most investments are little more than a gamble on what will happen to the price of shares in the future.

GOVERNMENTS

The safest financial investments are generally agreed to be government bonds – the so-called gilt edged securities. These are financial contracts whereby individuals or institutions lend money to the government which pays a fixed rate of interest in return (see Chapter 6).

The ethical issues involved in lending money to the government are not dissimilar to those involved in placing money in a large multinational corporation. Governments, like large corporations, carry out many functions and your money could be used for any of them. Therefore if you do not want your money to be used for waging war, you should avoid government stocks as the money could be boosting the military budget. Similarly if you believe the police service is becoming too repressive, or you disagree with the working of MI5 or MI6, you would need to avoid government stocks to keep a clear conscience.

Conversely if you would like more money to go to overseas aid, or to boost the national health service, this might attract you to buying government bonds – but whatever your motivations, remember your money goes into a big pot and the politicians then decide what to do with it.

LARGE OR SMALL COMPANIES?

'Small is beautiful' is the rallying cry of the Greens. Investors attempting to decide whether to put their money into a large industrial conglomerate will quickly see why. The larger the company, the more fingers it has in more pies, and the more likely it is to be undertaking activities you will find unacceptable.

Many multinational companies see their route to expansion in buying other companies, and often the companies they buy are operating in an entirely different part of the market. A cynic might ask why a board of directors used to running a chemical works might suddenly feel they can run a chain of grocery shops, but such considerations seem to receive little attention in our company board rooms. However, for the ethical investor these continual take-overs make it difficult to know whether the company continues to fit your criteria.

Furthermore as companies get larger they gain a level of power which I and many people find disturbing: large companies have been known to threaten to close down factories unless a local council agrees to give them development grants; or a haulage company might threaten to reduce its donations to a political party unless the motorway network is expanded.

Smaller companies more often óperate in a local area, so the profits earned are mainly spent locally to benefit the local economy. Often the owners work on the shop floor and are not isolated from the workforce in a headquarters building far away. Large companies can employ technicians to make small but insidious changes to a product – so in supermarkets for instance, food technicians pump the artificial scent of baking bread to persuade customers to buy. Many shoppers are rightly cynical about such manoeuvres, but smaller businesses simply don't have the time to indulge in such malarkey and your investment money is more likely to be used for its core business.

Smaller businesses, too, can be set up as worker co-operatives, or sole traders. People then have much greater say over how they work, leading to greater job satisfaction, a more personal relationship with customers, and products which are more custom made.

Conversely, small companies can find it difficult to fund the research needed to improve products, or introduce new ones, particularly where high technology is involved. They are also unable to take advantage of economies of scale, and so customers may find they are having to pay more than they would if they bought from the larger competitor.

Small companies are usually viewed as a high (financial) risk by the conventional investment world, which in turn means they find it more difficult to obtain investment funding.

MILITARY

While the world's armed forces are (generally) government-run, the production of weapons and associated equipment is mostly in private hands. Governments encourage these companies to sell their weaponry across the world with the argument that it makes the production 'more economic' if they are not just reliant on a single customer.

While few people need to be convinced of the awfulness of war; the argument that preparing for war increases its likelihood is unfortunately not universally accepted. Governments attempt to regulate the sales of armaments by specifying they shouldn't go to regimes which appear to be exacerbating the chance of war. This amounts to them saying that weapons shouldn't be sold to anyone likely to actually *use* them. This is clearly absurd, and in recent years British soldiers have been fighting armies equipped with weapons supplied by UK companies.

Furthermore many weapons sold by British companies are not actually designed to be used against foreign aggressors – they are for use against a country's own populace. Other weapons such as land mines play a comparatively small part in a war, but remain in the ground afterwards to maim and kill civilians with devastating effect.

Purchasing of armaments by countries also dramatically affects the amount of money available to boost the standards of living of ordinary people. Many economists attribute the economic success of Germany and Japan to the restrictions placed on their armed forces, while a contributor to the UK's economic malaise is the high proportion of spending on 'defence'.

In the Third World, the issues are even more acute, where governments are able to show off expensive tanks, helicopter gunships, high technology rifles and jet aircraft while many of the populace don't have access to sufficient clean water, clothing, shelter and food.

The difficulty for politicians who genuinely want to wage peace by reducing spending on the military is the pressure brought to bear by the 'defence' industry on the grounds of the resulting loss of jobs and damage to the economy.

I believe that if I invest in the armaments industry, my money will increase the chances of war and the death and destruction which comes in its wake.

OPENNESS

Freedom of information about a company's activities is vital for customers, workers, suppliers and investors. Despite all these groups having an interest in a company's operation, all a business is actually required to reveal are some very limited statements and figures in its annual report to the Department of Trade. Particular industries have to declare certain other information – for example food producers have to declare ingredients on their products – but in the main the amount of information available is tiny.

Directors use the catch-all defence of 'commercial confidence' as an excuse to restrict the release of virtually all other information. An indication of the importance of the information kept under wraps is the uproar which ensues when documents are leaked or released without authority. If investors had known earlier about the affairs of the Bank of Credit and Commerce International, they might have lost less money. Similarly, members of the Mirror Group Newspapers pension scheme might have been able to protect their pensions if they had been aware of Robert Maxwell's unauthorised use of the money. If the public had known of the safety standards adopted at the Bhopal chemical plant in India, the huge release of toxic fumes could have been avoided.

OPPRESSIVE REGIMES

When far-sighted church leaders became concerned about their money going to countries operating in South Africa, ethical investment as a concept was born. Since then, South Africa has returned to democracy, but sadly many other countries are still run by governments which recognise few human rights.

Reports of killings and torture in Nigeria and Indonesia should be enough to persuade investors not to place their money with companies operating there. Long sentences on political prisoners in Burma, Tibet and China should rule these countries out. Other countries with high military expenditures (which often have high levels of poverty too) should also be excluded.

Foreign companies operating in such countries often plead that their investment helps local people, or that they have no direct involvement in the sins of the government. Nevertheless outside investment often gives a governing elite access to hard currency which bolsters their power, while a country with no access to world markets is likely to become unstable, thus making the position of the government precarious.

Ethical savers will find such investments highly troubling to the conscience.

PRODUCTS

Products come onto the market only if they are likely to return a profit. Whether a product contributes to human welfare is barely an issue for most companies, and whether it gives pleasure or benefits the customer at the expense of others is also hardly on the agenda at most board meetings. Even environmental impact is scarcely considered.

Yet I believe these are perfectly reasonable questions to ask about the work of our companies, and it is only right that ethical investors should ask them. Is it justified to produce cars which can be driven at double the speed limit, squandering fuel, contributing to global warming, and endangering other road users?

Similarly, is it right to produce goods which have a limited lifespan, and which are very expensive to repair? Is the company doing the community a good service by using a surplus of packaging which ostensibly makes the product more attractive, but which will cause pollution when disposed of, and will contribute to high council taxes as local authorities bear the cost of disposal?

Such issues should be considered by investors before deciding to invest – all are vitally important, and all can affect the welfare of the people using the products, and the environment which will suffer from pollution and waste of resources.

PROFIT

The ethical issues surrounding profits concern whether profit is the principal aim of the business, or whether some form of social benefit is the company's *raison d'être*. With the growth of trading organisations in the 'social economy' there's a realisation that it is often better for work to be done because the resulting product or service is needed than because the profit is wanted.

An example is to be found in the high street banks whose main purpose *should* be to help people manage and store their money. Yet many banks are now earning more money from speculating on the derivatives markets (which barely benefit anyone) than from providing the banking services which people need. To make matters worse, banks are withdrawing from poor areas because they can't make enough there to justify maintaining branches, and are pushing people to stop using money in the form of cash and coin altogether. (At least one major bank does not provide a facility for employees to buy lunch in the staff canteen with cash – they have to use debit cards.)

Companies such as Traidcraft PLC exists primarily to give people in the Third World an avenue for fair trading. The Centre for Alternative Technology which is also now a public company exists primarily to advance the cause of alternative technology. For these two companies – and there will undoubtedly be more in the future – profit is a secondary consideration to their primary reason for existence. It is not that such companies do not care whether they make a profit or a loss. Rather, their primary use for profits is to aid their primary function, rather than to line the pockets of outside investors.

Is unearned income ever ethical?

The issue of whether it is ethical to profit from investing money at all has been much discussed. The question goes far beyond the socialist view, according to which it is fundamentally wrong for people to receive income merely because they have spare cash to invest, because their profit comes off the backs of the workers.

For most of us, the balance is between how much profit we are making from our investment, and how much those doing the physical work are getting. If you are receiving a high return because the company you invest in runs a factory in China using virtual slave labour, you should question your conscience very hard. If on the other hand your profit is only a small amount over the inflation rate, and the company is making socially useful products and the employees enjoy working there, you can probably receive your income without any qualms.

In a more esoteric vein we may ask what harm interest as such is doing to our economy. It is rarely asked whether paying and receiving interest is itself ethical. There is some evidence that the payment of interest is a principal contributor to our ever expanding economy and the resulting environmental degradation.

The view is held because most companies expand their work by borrowing cash, and on this cash they are paying interest. These payments for using money means they have to expand more than they would otherwise: and therefore attempt to sell more of their product, and use up more energy to make and sell it than they would do if the money for expansion was available without an interest charge. This affects individuals who in turn have to work more to earn the interest component of the products they buy (the real sum paid for a house can be three times as much as the sale price when interest payments are taken into account).

At the heart of the matter is the way money comes into existence at all. In the UK, a maximum of 15% of the money in circulation is notes and coin manufactured by the government. The rest exists in the form of figures in accounts which change as people and organisations spend and receive money. The *amount* of this money in circulation is continually increasing because it is the banks which create it by earning interest when they lend it out.

Imagine we are starting the economy from new, and the total money in it is £100 in cash in the hands of one individual. The individual deposits the £100 in the bank, the bank can lend out perhaps 90% or more of it to other customers. The banks can do this because they know that at any one time only about 10% of their money will be demanded back by depositors. Thus £90 is lent to another customer (with interest charged by the bank) and the borrower uses it to buy some goods, the seller of which then deposits the £90 paid back in the bank. According to the bank's records, the £100 in our economy has now increased to £190 plus the interest earned by the bank. The bank can now lend out 90% of this £90 to another customer, and the amount of money in circulation increases further. Each of these people who borrowed the money is charged interest which they have to earn, and which is paid to the bank, which can then lend it out afresh. The extra money being created is the difference between the rate of interest charged by the banks on loans compared with the amount they pay to depositors.

Consequently the banks are for ever seeking fresh customers to lend money to, and the amount of money in the economy is continually expanding. As money is lent, those who borrow it need to produce more goods and services to pay back the loan and the interest charged.

Thus ethical depositors who are concerned at environmental damage being caused by increasing amounts of industrial production need to consider whether it is indeed ethical to seek the highest interest return on their money.

RELIGION

While most companies will try to sell to all comers and accept investments from anyone, some are closely connected with particular religious groups. Sometimes the directors come from a particular religion, in other cases fringe religions have started up businesses to bring money into their coffers.

Only a few companies are involved, and if you are a strong believer in a particular religion, you may want to consider whether a company has close attachments to a different religious grouping – and whether this is sufficient justification for you not to invest with them. Alternatively, you may wish to choose a company that shares your own religious or church affiliation.

SOUTH AFRICA

The question of whether to invest in South Africa has now moved full circle. The new black majority government is actively appealing for Western investors.

Ethical investors should heed this advice, but should also consider whether they want to invest in the companies which busied themselves in South Africa during the period of apartheid. It would not do these companies any harm to be made aware that they will lose some investment income because of their uncaring attitude during those years.

TOBACCO

Tobacco is one of the few products which cause serious and possibly fatal illness when used in accordance with the manufacturers' 'instructions'. Despite industry protestations, most medical practitioners agree that smoking can lead to lung cancer. In addition, tobacco's addictive qualities mean that once a person is hooked on tobacco, they find it difficult to give up. For many people the addiction begins very young. Recent evidence indicates that passive smoking – being in the presence of smokers and breathing in their smoke – can also lead to lung cancer.

Cigarette companies have seen sales fall or stabilise in Western countries as the practice becomes more unpopular and have switched their marketing strategy to the Third World where there are few if any restrictions on sales to children, and little education about the damage smoking can cause.

Recent evidence also indicates that repeated growing of tobacco causes serious soil degradation, which will cause further poverty and desertification in the Third World countries where it is grown as a cash crop.

No simple matter

The huge range of issues to be considered when making an investment in a business can be seen from this hypothetical example. As the tale of imaginary companies A and B unfolds investors will see the difficulties and how their money can be used for social good or something very different.

Two imaginary companies are inviting your investment to expand their production of wooden dining chairs. Company A wants the money to buy another furniture maker. Company B wants the money to buy 50 acres of woodland. Which would you invest with?

Cartoon courtesy of the New Economics Foundation

Company A is a transnational corporation with factories, distributors and retailers in 27 different countries. Their dining chairs division is only one sector in a diverse set of interests spanning car production, electricity generating, investment and property companies, an electronics division, and cigar making. Their headquarters are in Liechtenstein, and they operate several factories in countries on the Pacific rim and more recently have been accused of operating at one of the 'slave camps' in mainland China.

Their dining chair production involves cutting mixed hardwood trees in Brazil and transporting the cut timber to Malaysia where it is shredded to make chipboard. The glue for bonding is made in Indonesia where environmental regulations regarding disposal of waste chemicals from the process are notoriously lax. The chipboard is shaped in Malaysia in a factory where trade unions are forbidden, no sick pay is available, and the average working week is 85 hours, giving a wage of approximately £185 pa.

The shaped parts are exported by ship to Poland where they are assembled into completed chairs, packed in polystyrene, and then trucked in 44 tonne lorries across Europe to one of the company's large do-it-yourself hypermarkets three miles outside your town. The hypermarket employs large numbers of part-time workers who have little knowledge of the goods available, and who are quietly told it would be in their interest to work at least one Sunday in three. Customers who have bought the chairs have discovered that joints have opened and legs broken within three years of purchase, and there are no repair facilities available.

Company B comprises five people who have rented a woodland on the opposite side of your town. They have set up as traditional chair bodgers in the wood, though they have brought the craft up to date by using electric tools powered by a wind turbine they installed in a field nearby. The chairs are fashioned entirely in the wood, and they have an agreement with a craft worker nearby who makes glues from animals which have died naturally.

The chair bodgers were quite prepared to use a van to deliver their products, but one of their number is very fond of horses, and combines business with pleasure by keeping a pair of driving horse and a cart available for deliveries. The cart doubles as an effective advertising medium and is also used to bring local children to the woods to learn how the chairs are made.

Hard-headed financiers would recommend putting your money into company A since their diverse interests, publicly available shares, and low unit costs are more likely to produce a higher investment return. They would be likely to regard company B as a high risk hobby business which is all very nice but hardly relevant to the real world as the likelihood is that their chairs would be too expensive to attain volume sales.

Yet, if you wanted your money to be used well in the long term, you would be advised to avoid company A like the plague – the damage to people and the environment from their processes should not rest easily on anyone's conscience; while company B could continue making chairs no matter what happens to the economy.

POLITICS

Business people will often plead that they are not involved in politics: they are involved in business. Yet how businesses conduct themselves vis à vis the political system has a great influence on how well that system functions.

At its simplest the large amount of money given by companies to the UK Conservative Party influences how extensively they can put their message across to voters at election time. Such close political connections might lead to other arrangements which investors might find unacceptable – for example governments watering down legislation which might benefit the population but harm the financial interests of a donor company.

More insidiously, the flow of money and factories abroad destabilises a government trying to wrest control of the country's financial affairs.

Transnational companies particularly examine how repressive a regime is before deciding whether to invest. Pressure groups and social researchers have often revealed how a company will open a factory in a country with a repressive government because they will be able to pay lower wages where the workforce will be unable to form a strong trade union to balance their power. Similar investment decisions may be made because environmental regulations are less strict and a company could emit pollutants which wouldn't be countenanced in a more democratic country.

Business activities in many countries with repressive regimes can lead to other unacceptable activities. In recent years several British companies have had the spotlight of public disapproval turned on them for bribing government officials in return for contracts. Sometimes such contracts are wholly unsuitable for the country, or are overturned later. In the days of President

Marcos of the Philippines, officials ordered a nuclear power station. Now that Marcos has departed, the power station has never operated (something most of us should be thankful for) but the country has to still pay back the loan they were granted for it by Western banks.

PORNOGRAPHY

As women have campaigned for equality opportunities across the whole gamut of society, much attention has been focused on the production of pornographic films, videos, and magazines. The concern is that images of women as sex objects available to be exploited reinforces men's notions that this is how women are to be treated.

While many subscribe to this view, others are concerned about defining what is pornographic and degrading. Others again are concerned about issues such as freedom of speech, while yet others believe that such is the male psyche that the availability of pornography may reduce the number of violent sexual crimes. Whichever view you take, it is important to realise that these issues are rarely in the mind of those producing pornography: their interest is only to make money. Ethical investors have a higher aim than this – that their money contributes to human or environmental welfare.

STAKEHOLDERS

The work of companies affects many different groups of people – the work-force, suppliers, customers, the local community and shareholders – known collectively as 'stakeholders'. Many multinational corporations now have annual turnovers in excess of those of many countries, and certainly in excess of many local governments, so the effect on stakeholders can be considerable.

The likelihood is that you will find yourself a stakeholder in a wide variety of businesses, and so you will see at first hand how the companies treat you.

Traditionally, companies have treated the customer as most important, the shareholder as not quite so important, and the other groups far down the list, or perhaps not on it at all.

Yet how these groups relate to the company is vitally important, and investors considering placing their money in a company should have a high regard to how these various stakeholders are treated. A company which is cavalier about the health and safety of its workers, for instance, is not deserving of your money. Similarly, a company which makes most of its profits in your town but gives nothing substantial back to the community should be avoided. (A litmus test of a company's interest in the surrounding community is whether they are funding facilities likely to be of interest mainly to the company's owners – such as donations to the golf club for instance – or whether help is being given to comparatively unpopular causes such as unemployed people or the homeless).

5

Green issues by industrial sector

● ●

'We have reached the limits to growth: it is over-production and over-consumption that is causing the planet's serious resource and environmental problems. We are already short of resources and are destroying the environment. If we maintain 4 per cent growth for 70 years, annual output will be 16 times as big as now, and if all the people in the world rise to the per capita income levels the rich countries would have then, world output would be 220 times as great as it is now'.
Ted Trainer, *Towards a Sustainable Economy*, 1996.

THE STOCK MARKET and financial press group the daily share prices of companies according to the type of business being undertaken.

The different sectors obviously have differing environmental impacts – a chemical company will affect people and the environment in a very different way from the retail industry. Here we look at the environmental impact of the principal industrial sectors. Investors who are only concerned about profit should examine these environmental impacts very carefully – for although there is little strategic information available as yet, all these environmental effects will have a financial cost, and those costs are likely to influence profitability and share prices in the years to come.

In 1995 economists and environmentalists began talking of 'negative asset value', the idea that the cost of a company's environmental liabilities exceeds its financial wealth. According to Joe Tanega, an academic from the Kingston Business School, UK industry could face such liabilities of tens of billions of pounds, none of which currently appear on company accounts.

A study by the US-based Investor Responsibility Research Centre in mid 1995 concluded that poor environmental performance is closely linked with lower company profits; and conversely, high environmental performances is linked with above average profitability. The three researchers, Mark Cohen, Scott Fenn and Jonathan Naimon constructed portfolios of equivalent firms but with good and poor environmental performances. They rated the companies on a range of issues including ownership of polluted land, number and cost of fines for breaking environmental regulations, and the volume and number of chemical and oil spills. The study concluded:

> In more than 80 per cent of the portfolio comparisons, the 'low pollution' portfolio performs better than the 'high pollution' portfolio. Firms with a relatively large number of environmental lawsuits as compared to their industry cohorts were found to earn a lower level of return on assets and return on equity. Companies with a low number [of contaminated sites] outperformed the 'high site' portfolio. The return on assets and return on equity are generally lower for companies in the high oil spill portfolio. The differences are quite large and statistically significant.

The report goes on to list similar findings in most of the other factors they considered.

However, ascertaining the financial cost of environmental risk is still in its infancy. Major investors such as the financial institutions (see Chapter 7) tend to react in a fairly unsophisticated way to environmental scare stories and pollution accidents.

Even some organisations which think themselves at the cutting edge of such matters have far to go. The Centre for the Study of Financial Innovation, for example, has proposed an Environmental Risk Rating which would operate similarly to credit ratings: that is, companies would be graded according to the environmental risk their activities face and the abilities of the management to address them. In their proposals, the CSFI state: 'The concept of sustainable development which has become central to an environmental outlook features little in stockbrokers' circulars (if it did, markets would be slumping, not booming.)' This reference to 'slumping', coming as it does in brackets almost as an aside, was echoed when the Centre did a pilot study of their Rating on Scottish Nuclear. The result of the assessment was that this nuclear company earned the rating 'A', the third lowest risk, described as 'A company with large but well identified environmental liabilities, and sufficient financial and management strength to absorb all but exceptional risks. Able, also, to finance any currently proposed regulatory requirements'. Many environmentalists would query such a verdict, not least because nuclear waste from such power stations remains radioactive for thousands of years, and that the study revealed that Scottish Nuclear invested the money they were supposedly putting aside to finance the decommissioning of their stations back into their company, rather than keeping it invested elsewhere. These two issues alone should have suggested that the risk rating for this nuclear companies should have been much more more severe.

The nuclear industry is one of the industries at the centre of controversy over environmental impact, but other sectors have their problems too. Let us look at some of the uses to which our money is put when we make a conventional investment...

BEVERAGES

The worldwide soft drinks market has spawned some of the most well known trade names and has contributed to a growing 'monoculture' across national and regional frontiers. Most household branded drinks are produced by large multinational companies, and the environmental impact includes the transport of large amounts of liquids, the number of containers which are neither re-used nor recycled, and the effect of large plantations growing the raw materials, particularly in the developing world. The marketing of alcoholic drinks can lead to alcoholism, while the consumption of carbonated drinks among the poor (and others) can be an unhealthy and expensive way of alleviating feelings of hunger.

BUILDING AND CONSTRUCTION

The use of materials such as gravel, lead, tropical hardwoods, and CFC blown materials contribute significant quantities of pollution. 50% of CO_2 emissions from fossil fuels comes from generating energy for heating buildings, and 50% of CFCs are for use in air conditioning and insulation. The manufacture of materials uses high amounts of energy and produces considerable quantities of toxic metals. The construction industry has a poor accident record among its workforce compared with other industries.

CHEMICALS

The chemical industry uses 21% of the world's energy and produces 58% of its toxic releases. Disasters such as those at Seveso, Bhopal, and Basel indicate a poor standard of care and attention in the industry. The release of chemicals has been linked with deformed fish and reduced breeding success among birds. Beluga whales off the Canadian coast have been technically classified as toxic waste. The industry produces 100,000 chemicals every year and develops a further 1000 making supervision difficult, a problem exacerbated by the complexity of the processes involved. There are some 500 separate processes involved in petrochemical manufacture alone.

Some companies see the Third World as a free dumping ground for waste, and many chemicals illegal in the UK are sold in the Third World without restriction.

A considerable amount of animal testing is carried out by the industry.

ELECTRONICS AND ELECTRICALS

The average UK home has 23 mains electrical appliances and six battery powered items. Most fridges use ozone depleting chemicals, and much waste in the industry is hazardous and rarely recycled. The common use of solvents leads to pollution, and the manufacturing process for many electrical items causes extensive water pollution. The average computer work station uses 33,000 litres of water in manufacture.

Electronic radiation in offices and from microwave ovens is only beginning to be understood. The defence industry is a major customer of this sector.

ELECTRICITY

The generating of electricity causes acid rain, nuclear radiation, CO_2 emissions contributing to climate change, and photochemical smogs caused by NOx and hydrocarbons. The UK is the fourth largest producer of SOx and the fifth largest of NOx. Electromagnetic radiation from power lines has been linked with cancer.

EXTRACTIVE INDUSTRIES

While steel, copper, lead, tin and aluminium are the main materials recycled, the industry is still a major contributor to CO_2 emissions and the greenhouse effect. Metal working requires large amounts of energy mainly from electricity and fossil fuels.

Sulphur dioxide emissions lead to acid rain, while mercury, cadmium, lead and zinc are highly toxic in manufacture.

Six million tons of solid waste such as clinker are landfilled annually with waste being exported to countries such as Brazil, Bolivia and the Philippines. Mining is the industry producing the most waste of any sector – some 108 million tons per annum.

Strip mining, reliance on heavy lorries, and water table disruption have all brought their own environmental problems. The industry has also been at the centre of allegations of price fixing and running cartels.

FINANCE

The financial industry is one of the most powerful in the world. The 160 partners of Goldman Sachs earned more in 1993 than the whole of Tanzania. The sector funds much environmental damage through its lending or ownership of shares. Their failure to properly assess environmental risk is leading to banks and insurance companies facing ever growing claims for damages with resultant losses.

Banks are the holders of much Third World debt (see Chapter 8). They also own extensive stretches of agricultural land and their demand for profits is a driving force in intensive agriculture.

FOOD

Large companies dominating the food market have lead to a demand for bulk quantities which in turn requires large farm holdings. This has resulted in a decrease in biodiversity, increased water pollution from farm effluent and chemicals, deterioration of soil and loss of access to land. Transport of food and extensive packaging leads to extensive pollution, while the use of CFCs in fridges and freezers is contributing to ozone depletion.

People's health is effected by over-consumption, poor diets, chemical additives and food irradiation. Factory farming keeps animals in inhumane conditions, while farmers suffer one of the highest suicide rates.

FORESTRY

Millions of acres of forest are being destroyed by commercial logging. Deforesting leads to soil erosion and estuary damage as soil flows downstream. In the Third World there has been forcible expropriation of land to establish plantations. Chemical treatment of timber affects workers.

GENERAL RETAILING

Large stores promote many unnecessary purchases through store design. The sale of tropical hardwoods are a major cause of forest destruction while solvents in materials cause water and air pollution. Few shops incorporate energy efficiency in their design.

LEISURE AND HOTELS

Tourism is the one of the world's biggest industries, turning over £3.5b annually and employing 1 in 15 workers worldwide. The industry is responsible for huge amounts of land, through travel facilities, hotel development, and theme parks. Pressures on basic infrastructure increase as large numbers of visitors arrive, leading to sewage and water supply problems. Many 'free' products in hotels are ultra disposable, while souvenirs such as coral, shells and stuffed animals endanger many species. Tourism causes considerable impact on local peoples and cultures leading in some extremes to the spread of disease and sex tourism and forcible removal of peoples from their land.

OIL AND GAS

Many vulnerable habitats are endangered by oil and gas exploration, including rainforests and oceans. Thousands of chemicals are used in the production of gas and oil and disposal is often unregulated.

Oil and gas extraction companies have been gradually moving from heavily regulated areas such as the US to less regulated Third World countries – at least 100 refineries in the US have closed since 1981 with substitutes opening in China, India, Thailand, Romania and Egypt.

Waste materials (including cadmium, cobalt, iron, mercury, nickel, platinum, silver and vanadium) have led to large areas of contamination on land and the seabed.

PHARMACEUTICALS

The continuing drive for new health treatments leads to the marketing of ever more drugs with resultant side effects and pollution. The sector is very heavily regulated and wastes tend to be of low volume but high toxicity, so small spillages cause disproportionate damage to health and the environment.

The Sandoz fire at Basel caused a 25 mile long stream of pollution in the River Rhine. There is considerable controversy over the use of animals for testing drugs, with some scientific opinion suggesting that the results from such tests are less than reliable. There is also deep concern about the patenting of genetic materials and organisms.

Tranquillisers are addictive, and many drugs produce unwanted side effects, among the worst being those resulting from Thalidomide.

PRINTING, PAPER AND PACKAGING

The production of paper is relatively energy intensive and polluting. In the US, this sector uses 11.5% of the country's energy and produces 13.5% of its toxic releases. Primary forests in Ghana, the Ivory Coast, Central African Republic, Nigeria, Tanzania and Indonesia have been logged for paper following overcapacity in the industry which has led to tree cutting in the cheapest countries. Paper production also uses large amounts of water. Items such as nappies, sanitary towels, and toilet paper are being dumped into the seas and estuaries and ending up on beaches. There is concern over the chlorine bleaching of women's sanitary products.

TEXTILES

Textile production uses – and pollutes – large quantities of water. Working conditions of people in this sector in both the Third World and the industrialised countries are poor.

Cotton growing uses high amounts of pesticides and fertilisers, and wools have been found with residues from dipping. Artificial fibres rely on oil for their production and are not biodegradable. Dry cleaning uses ozone depleting chemicals and has been linked to cancer in the workforce. The never ending changes of fashion causes considerable waste as clothes are discarded before they wear out.

TRANSPORT

Energy consumption by transport is causing global warming, acid rain, photochemical smog, and carbon monoxide. Air travel is worst per passenger mile of all transport types and supersonic flights are believed to caused ozone depletion. Transport uses nearly a third of all the UK's energy.

Moving freight by road is environmentally inefficient – it is estimated that 30% of all cargo journeys have one leg empty.

Road building splits communities and uses considerable amounts of land. Many petrol stations have leaking tanks – Shell says one third of its stations have contamination problems. Roadside contamination includes deposits of toxic metals including lead, zinc and cadmium. The popularity of 'just-in-time' deliveries has resulted in numerous short trips.

Ships are the world's largest human-made structures and have a history of oil spills, rubbish thrown overboard and waste water production – the QE2 generates 5 tons of waste water each day.

WATER

Most sewage receives little or no treatment before being deposited in estuaries or the sea. While much sewage is domestic in origin substantial amounts of toxic metals are released to the sewers by industry and agriculture.

In 1992 there were 31,680 water pollution incidents in England and Wales. As drinking water quality has declined, the demand for bottled water has increased with additional environmental impacts from transport and packaging.

6

Investing in the stock market

● ●

'With total honesty and strict adherence to the law, it is quite possible for the same accountants to draw up a balance sheet as highly profitable or in debt. Simply by deciding whether income should be described as profit, or placed in the reserves column, or carried forward to the following year, or set against an earlier loss, the image desired may be achieved'.

Tom Bower, *Maxwell, The Outsider*, 1988.

THE MAJORITY OF money from small investors which is not in building societies finds its way eventually to companies and other investments quoted on the Stock Exchange.

Some 2000 companies are quoted in the UK, although only about 650 are regularly traded. This small number of companies shows how concentrated industrial power has become: for although there are many more firms whose shares are not on sale to the public, most money is being invested in a very small number of businesses with huge turnovers.

The other investments quoted on the Stock Exchange mostly consist of local and central government bonds which pay fixed interest rates and can be cashed in after a specified period of time.

The return on most investments is thus reliant on how these companies perform: the level of their profits will determine whether investors receive sizeable dividends or losses. Ultimately, the performance of these companies determines the strength of the economy, and they therefore indirectly affect the government bonds too.

While large sums of money from small investors end up in these public companies, much of it arrives there after following fairly circuitous routes. It may have been put into a pension plan, life assurance or used to buy unit trusts; it may have gone through an investment trust, or just be in an ordinary bank account (see Chapters 7 and 8). Such financial contracts are marketed by the large city institutions, and their principal benefit is that they spread the investors' financial risk and take advantage of tax exemptions.

Quoted companies

'Quoted companies' are companies whose shares are available for sale to the general public and listed for resale on the Stock Exchange. As the name implies, a share in a company means that the investor *owns a share in it*, and that gives an entitlement to part of the profits and the risk of sharing in any losses, and a limited right to exercise some influence over how the company does its business (see Chapter 11).

While the shares of all PLCs are available to the public, it is only those listed on the Stock Exchange which can be readily bought and sold.

Underwriting the launch

When companies first create their shares it is considered essential that all the shares offered are sold on the first day they are available. This is because companies daren't take the risk that at the high profile launch their shares might appear to be not worth buying – and therefore the company is not an attractive investment. Companies try to ensure all shares are sold by pricing them somewhat lower than they think they are worth, so that investors are tempted to buy with the thought of a quick resale for profit. They also arrange for large financial institutions to *underwrite* the issue of shares and buy any that are not sold in the stock market itself. This is standard practice in the financial markets and there are hardly any new share issues which are not thus underwritten. But a detached observer might wonder why the issue of paper documents such as shares should *always* be underwritten, whereas the launch of a new *product* by a company is *never* underwritten. It is one of the many small signs which show that our economy pays more regard to the making of money out of money, than to the use of money to allow the exchange of goods and services which people need. New launches of shares from unquoted companies – such as those in the social economy (see Chapter 9) – are also never underwritten.

Companies seek stock market listings to raise cash for expansion or so the owners can raise cash for their own benefit,and by doing so, they are offering to share the ownership of the company with outside investors. The process involves creating more shares which are then sold. The Stock Exchange Council supervises this process to ensure the value of the shares created reflects the value of the company.

While the company will receive what the *first* buyers of the newly created shares pay for them, any subsequent sales of shares do not profit the company directly at all: the profit is made by the owners of the shares.

This subsequent buying and selling of shares constitutes the main activity of the Stock Exchange, and the argument for it is that investors will be unlikely to buy shares from companies in the first place if they do not have an easy way to sell them on in the future – when they want to use their money differently. The argument against this so-called secondary trading is that it does not actually contribute directly to the health of the companies involved or the economy at large, and that much trading is for short term profits and based on rumour and counter-rumour of how a company is doing. Unless you buy shares when they are first issued, your money will go to another investor rather than being used directly by the company whose business you wish to support.

All share deals are notified to the Stock Exchange Council and the continuous compilation of the number of sales causes the prices to continually rise and fall. Most of the profits and losses on the Stock Exchange are made from buying shares when they are cheap and selling them when the price rises – and vice versa.

Although a company is not directly affected if its share price falls, there are a number of potential knock-on effects. A company with a falling share price may find banks calling in loans or refusing to grant new ones, suppliers may refuse credit because they fear the company may go under and they would not get paid, or customers might refuse to buy if, for example, they feared spare parts might not be available if the company went into liquidation.

Shares of publicly quoted companies can be bought through banks, stockbrokers, or share shops and there are two prices: the higher one you pay for a share when you buy, and the lower one you receive when you sell. The difference is the dealer's overheads and profit.

Fair comment?

Although rumour and counter rumour play a large part in determining the price of shares, it is far easier for reports *favourable* to a company to circulate than those *critical*. The reason is the pervasive influence of the laws of defamation. An individual, or more relevantly, a publication which defames a person or a corporation – 'lowering their reputation in the eyes of reasonable people generally' – has to prove that what they have said is true. Corporations quoted on the Stock Exchange have great financial clout and often employ their own lawyers: thus it is easy for them to threaten legal action against publications and pressure groups which are publicly critical.

1995 saw the start of one of Britain's longest running libel trials when two Greenpeace London protesters were sued by the hamburger chain McDonalds for libel after they wrote a leaflet connecting the company with cutting down of the rainforest – an allegation McDonalds have repeatedly denied. In Austria the head of the country's largest electricity company took a Greenpeace campaigner to court for defamation because he had said that building a new coal-fired power station was tantamount to wilfully killing people because of the additional deaths which would result from the greenhouse effect. The Austrian campaigner won, but at the time of writing the critics of McDonalds were still in court.

Such cases, and as importantly, the *threat* of such cases, cause critics to be generally circumspect in their public statements. Preparing a case to back up such statements can be beyond the resources of pressure groups and many publications. It also needs to be remembered that there are broadly three interest groups analysing companies. Financial analysts often work for well funded institutions which are only concerned about the financial prospects. Pressure groups may be interested in a company's activities in certain areas, but they are usually poorly funded and reliant on public donations, and they can often only examine a fraction of the business world. Finally, journalists will seek out particular scandals while the financial pages generally report on profits and losses. Thus much concern about the damaging workings of companies is muted, and investors will only hear only a small amount of criticism of companies compared to favourable or non-committal comment.

Nevertheless when critical comment is published, share prices can react very quickly. A former colleague of the author now working for Reuters (which distributes considerable volumes of financial news) said much of his job satisfaction came from writing stories which are flashed around the world and result in changes to share prices within hours.

Thus investors need to be confident that the rise in the share price will more than offset the dealer's margin or that the dividend payment – the shareout of the profit – will compensate.

The share prices of fully quoted companies are published on the financial pages of daily newspapers. The newspapers quote the prices of these companies by grouping them into different industrial sectors (see Chapter 5 for more information on the environmental characteristics of each sector).

The conventional wisdom in the financial world is that individual investors need to have over £50,000 to invest before buying shares in companies directly. The reason is that below this figure it is difficult to obtain a sufficient spread of investments through different companies and industrial sectors to guard against losses. In practice there are many people who own a few hundred shares in one company or another, but what you have to remember is that if all or most of the shares you own are in one company, you will lose some or all of your investment if the company's business deteriorates or it goes into liquidation.

Furthermore, in order to make a profit from buying shares you need to be able to make informed decisions as to what and when to buy, and what and when to sell. Your information is likely to come from the media and since shares prices are continually moving up and down, relying on media reports will mean you're nearly always buying or selling when everyone else is. Thus it is very difficult to get the best prices.

It is also difficult to make a rigorous appraisal of the ethical standards of the public companies. Apart from the wide range of issues that may concern you (see Chapters 4 and 5), companies are huge organisations with a wide range of activities, some of which you are likely to approve of, while others you might vehemently oppose. The company Ecover, for instance, blazed the trail in environmentally-friendly soaps and detergents at a time when the major companies in the field cared not a hack for green issues. Hence the company could be thought of as a suitable place to invest funds. But in the early 1990s they were bought out by the company Group 4, which provided guards for motorway building sites and attracted considerable criticism for their methods of treating anti-motorway protesters.

There is, however, clear evidence that company directors need a deeper understanding of how environmental and ethical issues affect their business. When the Institute of Environmental Managers first tested applicants for associate membership in Autumn 1995, they found that 'a very sizeable number lacked any significant grasp of the implications of the sustainability debate for their business at all'. According to IEM director Alexander Peckham, the applications produced some bizarre responses with one applicant saying that sustainable development 'meant staying ahead of the competition'. Interestingly the IEM found that candidates showing a good grasp of environmental issues were also the best performers overall, suggesting they were also the best managers.

Getting informed

As a prospective investor, you can either rely on gut feelings about a company's standards, a method which would be pooh-poohed by professional financial analysts, or you can research particular companies by examining their annual reports and consulting some of the pressure groups working in areas that concern you.

If you want a more informed view, the Ethical Investment Research Service (EIRIS) offers a screening service on a wide range of ethical issues for private investors. EIRIS sends detailed questionnaires to companies and financial institutions (see Chapter 7) and produces tables showing whether specific companies are involved in undesirable activities, operating in particular countries, or have been the subject of prosecutions for health and safety or environmental issues. It keeps issues under review and its standards are used as a benchmark within the ethical investment industry. They examine companies listed on the UK and other European Stock Exchanges, but do not at present extend their service worldwide. They also produce lists of financial advisers with some experience of ethical investment.

EIRIS operates by distributing questionnaires on positive and negative criteria to prospective investors. Companies are then screened according to the investors' replies, and tailor-made 'approved' lists are produced. In 1995 EIRIS surveyed companies on the following issues:

✗ Advertising: complaints upheld by the Advertising Standards Authority or Independent TV Commission.

✗ Alcohol: production or sale.

✗ Animal testing: for pharmaceuticals, cosmetics, toiletries, or their suppliers; undertakings not to test on animals.

✗ Basic necessities: manufacture or sale of products or services which are basic necessities.

✗ Community involvement: members of Business in the Community, the Per Cent Club, donations to charity or the community, employee secondment schemes, gifts in kind, payroll giving schemes.

✗ Electricity: complaints from customers, disconnection rate, poor performance.

✗ Environmental issues: environmental audits and statements, use of wave, solar, wind, or geothermal energy, sponsors of conservation projects.

✗ Equal opportunities: equal opportunities policy and training, high proportion of women and ethnic minorities in management, high maternity and paternity leave provision.

✗ Financial institutions: banks, insurance, fund managers.

✗ Fur: sale of fur products.

✗ Gambling: of any sort including the National Lottery.

✗ Greenhouse gases: fossil fuel extraction, refining or distribution; electricity generation or supply; manufacture of generating equipment; services to oil, gas or coal industry; operation of aircraft; airports; high users of electricity; manufacturing high energy use equipment or appliances.

✗ Health and safety convictions: convictions with fines on one or more occasions.

✗ Human rights: subsidiaries or associates operating in countries involved in extrajudicial disappearances or executions, torture, or the holding of prisoners of conscience.

✗ Intensive farming: poultry, pig, fish farm, abattoir, manufacturing or supplying intensive farming equipment, sale or processing of meat.

✗ Military: contracts with the Ministry of Defence in the last three years, sale or production of goods or services used by the military.

✗ Mining: any mining or quarrying.

✗ Nuclear power: equipment or services for nuclear plants, distribution or supply of nuclear-generated electricity.

✗ Ozone depleting chemicals: suppliers and users of aerosols, fire extinguishers, refrigerators, foam products and industrial solvents containing CFCs, suppliers of ozone depleting chemicals.

✗ Pesticides: manufacturers of pesticides.

✗ Political donations: political donations of varying amount in the last five years.

✗ Pollution convictions: convictions following prosecution by The Environment Agency.

✗ Pornography or adult films: publishing, printing or distribution of pornography, newspapers with photographs of topless women, films or videos which have been cut to obtain an 18 certificate, adult TV entertainment services.

✗ Public transport and bicycles: operators of bus, train or coach services, manufacturers of buses, rolling stock and bicycles.

✗ Roads: roadbuilding, manufacturers of cars and commercial vehicles, members of the British Road Federation, hirers of motor vehicles, major users of road vehicles, wholesale or retail distribution of petrol or diesel.

✗ Safety: manufacturers of products designed to save or protect life.

✗ Size: companies among the largest on the Stock Exchange as a whole or in their sector.

✗ South Africa: payment of below the minimum wages there, or refusal to give information on wages paid and black people employed; provision of training to black employees, high numbers of black staff in senior positions, investors in redevelopment industries, recognition of trade unions; companies operating there in the year before economic sanctions were lifted.

✗ Third World: extraction or growing of commodities in the Third World; owed debts; contravention of codes on marketing baby milk, pesticides, and pharmaceuticals; marketing tobacco; or operating in the poorest countries.

✗ Tobacco: production or sale of tobacco and associated products.

✗ Training and education: providers of education and training.

✗ Transnational interests: subsidiaries or associates in more than 10 countries.

✗ Tropical hardwood: retailers of joinery or timber, users in manufacturing, extracting, importing and processing, or operating in tropical regions, declarations not to use tropical hardwood.

✗ Waste disposal: involvement in recycling or disposal of waste.

✗ Water: exceeding official discharge consents for chemicals and other substances, and convictions.

✗ Water companies: number of complaints, high disconnection rates, high number of water quality incidents, sewage plants exceeding discharge limits, high water leakage rate.

The magazine *Ethical Consumer* also examines the record of companies and assesses their record on a wide range of activities.

These include:

✘ Oppressive regimes: countries criticised by Amnesty International for torture, extrajudicial executions or disappearances, prisoners of conscience, and 'frequent official violence against the public'. The countries are graded into two groups: (1). Afghanistan, Burma, Colombia, India, Indonesia, Iran, Iraq, Lebanon, Liberia, Mauritania, Morocco, Peru, The Philippines, Somalia, Syria and Turkey; and (2) Algeria, Angola, Bahrain, Brazil, China, Egypt, El Salvador, Guatemala, Haiti, Honduras, Israel, Jordan, Kenya, Kuwait, Mali, Mexico, Nepal, Nigeria, Papua New Guinea, Senegal, Sri Lanka, Sudan and Uganda.

✘ Trade union relations: problems of trade union recognition or commentators' criticism of particularly heavy-handed responses to industrial action.

✘ Wages and conditions: wages levels that may not be enough to live on, or dangerous working conditions.

✘ Land rights: criticism of specific instances where indigenous peoples have been removed from their lands to facilitate corporate operations.

✘ Environment: criticism for activities which pollute or damage the environment.

✘ Irresponsible marketing: marketing of products in a way that has been criticised as being detrimental to health, or marketing of products in a way that has been criticised for causing severe physical harm.

✘ Nuclear power: corporate involvement in mining of uranium, production or distribution of technology, or research into nuclear energy.

✘ Armaments: involvement in the manufacture or supply of weapons and/or other combat equipment.

✘ Animal testing: licence to vivisect or involvement in vivisection, or subscriber to the British Industrial Biological Research Association which carries out contract testing.

✘ Factory farming: use of intensive farming techniques which have been criticised by animal welfare campaigners and/or the supply of products or services which contribute to inhumane husbandry.

✘ Other animal rights: involvement in the production of meat, leather or fur, including companies providing essential supplies to the meat industry.

✘ Political donations: donations to a political party in the UK.

✘ Boycott call: indications that a boycott of the company has been requested.

The magazine also include a page of 'boycott news' listing the companies which are the target of ethical and environmental boycotts by pressure groups. These need to be treated with some caution as calls for boycotts from large groups such as Greenpeace can be very effective but they encourage the use of this form of action by very small groups. The result is that at any one time a large range of companies are the target of boycotts, but many of the pressure groups involved have only a small following, and thus the effect is reduced. One group even calls for consumers to boycott The Body Shop because of their particular way of assessing whether products have been tested on animals. One can't help feeling that the wide range of companies with no concern for animal rights whatever should be the target of wrath, rather than The Body Shop which takes animals rights seriously.

The Ethical Consumer, as its name implies, is mainly aimed at customers though its information can just as well be used by investors.

Labour Research, published by the Labour Research Department, concentrates on the industrial relations aspects of companies and is also a useful source of information.

A story of confidence

In theory the price of the shares of a company rises and falls according to how well it is trading: a company returning high profits will see its shares trading at a higher price. This is because investors are willing to pay more as they will be receiving more in dividends as the profits are shared out. In practice share prices are as dependent on expectations of how a company is doing, as on what is actually happening. The story of The Body Shop in 1994 illustrates the difficulties for both ethical and non-ethical investors assessing share prices.

The Body Shop is one of the very few companies on the Stock Exchange which regards its ethical stance as being as important as the profit it makes – perhaps even more so. Yet in mid 1994 the business and environmental world was swept by rumours that a US magazine was about to produce an article on The Body Shop suggesting its green and ethical stance was not as resolute in practice as its public statements suggested.

In response a large ethical fund in the US sold 50,000 Body Shop shares, and the rumours spread. Most ethical funds found the allegations unlikely, but fund managers were left in a difficult position. Their ethical principles should have led them to come to an informed view of The Body Shop after seeing the magazine article and considering the weight of evidence, but their financial concerns could have led them to sell Body Shop shares because such rumours – even if subsequently unsubstantiated – can cause the shares to quickly drop in value. Media reports at the time (upon which private investors are likely to rely) didn't indicate whether the first fund to sell was doing so because they were concerned that The Body Shop was not as green as they thought, or because they feared *the shares would drop in value* because other investors would be rapidly selling.

In the event the share price of The Body Shop fell before the article appeared, and recovered after that. The company made some changes to its mode of operation as a result of the controversy, and the ethical investment watchdog EIRIS (see above) gave the company a broadly clean bill of health.

Bonds

While shares constitute ownership of part of a company, bonds are the other type of investment – that is they are loans. But confusingly, bonds are talked about in the literature as being products for sale: people are invited to 'buy' bonds which earn interest.

When an individual approaches a bank or other lending institution to borrow money, it is the bank which sets the rate and the payback arrangements: the borrower takes or leaves the offer. However, when a large institution such as a pension fund, public company, or the government itself wishes to borrow money from small investors it does so by issuing bonds. These are simply certificates which are placed on 'sale' at a certain price, paying a certain interest rate, and with the sum paid being refundable at a specified date in the future. Hence with small investors lending to large institutions, it is the borrower setting the conditions, the opposite of what happens when ordinary folk go to the bank for a loan.

Bonds are issued by four different types of organisation:

Company bonds are issued by public companies when they want to raise cash but don't want to issue more shares. For the investor they are slightly less risky than owning shares, for if a company goes into liquidation, bond-holders are higher on the list of creditors, and the interest payments are sometimes linked to the success of the company. Bonds can be issued at a fixed interest rate so buyers know what the payout will be (unlike shares where the dividend depends directly on the company profits) but they won't know whether the bond remains the best deal because interest rates elsewhere are continually moving up and down and better or worse deals may be had elsewhere. Some bonds are linked to dividends, while others can be converted to shares at a specified time. Some bonds are traded on the Stock Exchange, and the prices are quoted on a daily basis in newspapers along with company shares.

The ethical issues involved in buying bonds are the same as those involved in buying company shares: investors need to assess the company's work to decide if it meets with their ethical criteria.

Investment bonds are investments offered by the financial institutions and work in a similar way to unit trusts (see Chapter 7). Money from the investor is spread around a number of different company shares and other investments such as government bonds, property etc. to spread the risk. There are a number of variants, with some linked to insurance policies which guarantee that a minimum sum is paid out in the event of, say, the investor's death. Some pay at a fixed interest, while others are tied to stock market performance.

Money used to buy an investment bond usually goes into the unit trust run by the institution which acts as the conduit to the company shares. But while there is a legal obligation for institutions to declare the exact mix of company shares owned by the unit trust, there is no such obligation for the sales of investment bonds. Investors are left to presume their money is being used as in the unit trust, but with no certainty. None of the institutions offering ethical investment bonds declares exactly where the investments are made.

Like all such mixed investments, you need to examine any ethical criteria adopted by the fund, and then examine the particular companies etc.(as best you can) in which the money is invested.

Central government bonds are bonds issued regularly by the government. They pay interest which is either fixed or fluctuates by being linked to inflation and with repayment being due at a specified date. Like company bonds, the resale prices fluctuate according to how the prevailing interest rate is moving, and the prices are quoted in daily newspapers. The risk of losing your money in government bonds is generally viewed as very small: governments don't go into liquidation in the way companies can. Therefore when the repayment date on the bond arrives, investors can be virtually certain of collecting their money. Thus government bonds are known as 'gilt edged securities': the safest there are.

The money invested in government bonds goes to the Treasury, and thence to wherever the government needs it. Thus it is impossible for ethical investors to know what the funds are to be used for: they could be funding the health service or social security payments to the very poor; or they could be buying the next generation of nuclear weapons, paying the wages of MI5 agents spying on environmental organisations, or paying for the building of motorways through Sites of Special Scientific Interest. The only guide is the regular announcement by the Treasury of its entire spending plans. In 1995 these were: social security 28.5%, health 10.8%, environment 12.7%, education 3.6%, transport 1.4%, defence 7.1%, and other departments and debt payments 35.9%. Given that you can't specify a department when you invest, this is not much to go on.

Local government bonds operate in a similar way to central government bonds (see above). They are issued for particular councils, pay a fixed interest rate and are paid back by the issuer on a prescribed date. They are also quoted on the Stock Exchange and their price rises and falls, influenced by how long it is to their repayment date, and the general rate of interest in the economy.

Like central government bonds the money invested goes into the general accounts of the particular local council, but is used for capital expenses –

buildings and equipment – rather than revenue costs such as paying for rubbish collections. Local authorities engage in far fewer activities that ethical investors will find unacceptable, and in addition it is possible to invest in your own local authority if they have issued such bonds. Like company shares, however, if you don't buy the bond when it is first issued, your money is likely to go to profit another investor or speculator, rather than going direct to the council.

A small number of local authorities issue 'over the counter bonds' which can be bought direct from the councils themselves with the money raised used in the same way as the other bonds described above. These over the counter bonds are not traded on the Stock Exchange, pay a set rate of interest and the capital sum can be recovered by returning the bond to the issuing council.

Investment clubs

While individual investment directly in shares is seen as financially risky, and unit trusts have problems meeting people's very different ethical criteria, share clubs rest in the middle. These are small groups of investors who pool their money to invest directly in company shares or bonds. While the unit trusts make their decisions on where to invest using highly paid investment analysts, the members of share clubs make the decisions themselves. They do so by meeting regularly and assessing the strengths and weaknesses of companies in the same way as investors putting money directly into companies: by using any information available.

While the clubs are independent, they are supported by ProShare Investment Clubs, a non-profit making organisation funded by the Stock Exchange which provides detailed manuals on running the clubs. As far as is known, there are no ethical investment clubs, but there is no reason why a group of people with money to invest shouldn't form such a club and operate it according to whatever ethical criteria they choose. The advantage would be that they could invest according to the issues they believed were important, and the pooling of funds would spread some of the risk, but they would not have the benefit of professional fund managers continually assessing companies both for risk and ethical criteria.

Managed stockbroking

Stockbrokers are firms which buy and sell shares on behalf of individuals and institutions. They earn their money by charging a commission, and any individual investor wanting to buy shares in companies will buy them from a stockbroker (or bank offering a stockbroking service) who has in turn bought them from other investors.

Stockbrokers offer three different types of service: they will simply buy or sell blocks of shares according to instructions given by the investor; they will give advice to investors on likely trends in the market with suggestions as to what to buy or sell; or they will manage an investor's portfolio by buying and selling shares as they think fit, and send regular statements of what they've traded – and the resulting profits or losses. The two latter services are generally only on offer to investors with more than £50,000 or £100,000 to invest. Some stockbrokers are now starting to offer ethical broking services.

The stockbrokers Albert E. Sharp run such a service aimed at ethical investors directly and in conjunction with the financial advisers Holden Meehan (see Chapter 10). The service allows an individual investor to specify the ethical criteria they want incorporated and the stockbroker buys stocks and shares accordingly. Albert E. Sharp use the ethical criteria provided by EIRIS as the basis for their research. Once undesirable companies have been screened out, the A.E. Sharp ethical team seek companies fulfilling positive criteria.

Overseas investments

As trade has expanded into the global marketplace, so have the opportunities to invest in overseas companies. Green and ethical investors face particular problems with overseas companies, the principal one being knowledge of what companies are doing, and the particular business ethos to be found in a country. For example, many Japanese companies actively discourage or bar women from serving on their boards of directors – a position which many UK investors would find highly offensive.

Also, while many people do not rate the UK's environmental regulations very highly, they are far more stringent than those found in many other countries, and such investors should be opposed to the buying of shares in companies exploiting these legal discrepancies.

Gaining information on these companies is none too easy for small UK investors – even EIRIS only expanded its research beyond the UK to mainland Europe in 1995. There is little readily available research available on companies further afield and thus it is difficult for investors to review where fund managers are placing their money. Furthermore, shares sold on foreign stock exchanges are subject to widely different regulations – with some countries being notoriously lax while others are very stringent. Many ethical funds do however invest overseas and investors should grill the institutions about what exactly they know about the companies and the countries they operate in.

The Green movement has adopted the motto 'Think globally, act locally' – investors might consider this a useful rule of thumb when considering where to place their money.

7

Investing with the financial institutions in the stock market

• •

'The Rothschilds stopped buying and selling goods. They switched to the ultimate commodity. From 1810 on to this very hour, the family would buy and sell money only'.
Frederic Morton, *The Rothschilds*, 1964.

WHILE COMPANY SHARES and government bonds are the building blocks of investments, the various financial plans offered by the city institutions are the finished buildings: they come in a wide range of types, and the financial contracts they offer vary widely.

The institutions, be they pension funds, life offices, insurance companies or unit trust managers, take money from a wide range of investors and then spread it around shares, bonds, property, and various other financial instruments. The aim is to make financial returns commensurate with the risks being run and to take advantage of tax exemptions. Several institutions now offer ethical and green financial products and this is where most of the $1b of UK ethical investment is now placed.

A bewildering variety of financial products are available, and many investment plans weave together several different ones. Much of the work of the financial services industry involves merging together the different products.

Thus buying a pension will involve a unit trust, stockbroking, company shares, bonds, and an annuity. Life assurance is likely to include shares, government bonds and unit trusts. A Personal Equity Plan (PEP) can include company shares, unit trusts, investment trusts, bonds and stockbroking.

An ethical investor therefore has to exercise some diligence to make sure the various parts meet the required standard, while all investors need to work hard just to understand what return to expect, and how to calculate it.

But underlying the investments is the performance of companies: if company sales are high and costs low, profits from the different investment opportunities can be high, and of course vice versa. Underlying the companies, of course, is the environment itself: if the planet cannot support the stresses our industrial society places on it, then your investments will suffer – or worse may happen.

At the heart of the financial products are the unit trusts. Most of the investments offered by institutions – be they pensions, life assurance, or Personal Equity Plans – involve placing money in the unit trusts they run, but with other conditions added on.

The unit trusts

If companies fail to make sufficient profit, they may go into liquidation, and the shareholders then lose the money they spent on the shares. Although it is theoretically possible to purchase small numbers of shares in a company, because of dealing fees it is often not worthwhile to do so. Individual investors can thus take a high financial risk by buying shares direct.

Unit trusts were established to spread this risk and they work by pooling the money from many investors and then buying a wide selection of company shares and bonds. Thus if one company performs poorly or goes into liquidation, the effect is spread thinly among many people. (If *all* shares decrease in price because of a stock market crash, unitholders may suffer as much as direct investors.)

The unit trust managers make day by day decisions on where to invest, and the vast bulk of money will go into property, or securities listed on the stock market such as company shares, and government and corporate bonds (see Chapter 6).

The trusts publish details of their strategy and investments in their twice yearly reports, and potential investors can see exactly which companies the managers believe are likely to give a better return. The work involved in making these investment decisions is wrapped up in much mystique, and many managers are uncomfortable at the results of a survey which showed that only 43% of funds do better than the stock market average at investing – or to put it another way, most funds could invest indiscriminately in the largest 100 companies and perform just as well. Managers also need to be careful that they are not claiming to have special knowledge of the performance of companies, for they could face investigation for insider dealing if they have.

Investors considering buying into unit trusts should ensure they are given several recent managers' reports since these can give a somewhat different account of the performance than the brochure and application forms.

Like shares, there are two prices quoted for units in the trusts: the higher price is paid by investors when they buy units, and the lower is that received when investors want to sell. The difference constitutes the amount you pay the fund managers for setting up the fund, and the funds also charge an ongoing management fee of 1 – 2% per year of the total invested. The difference between the two prices tends to be greater in the ethical funds than in the mainstream unit trusts, reflecting the extra work involved in assessing companies' ethical performance. Unlike company shares, units can't be sold on to other investors, and can only be sold back to the unit fund managers who are obliged by law to buy them at the prevailing price. The price of the units rise and fall according to how well the underlying investments perform, and dividends can be paid in cash or by allocation of more units.

The trust's report will state whether it has under- or out-performed average share prices. An outperformance theoretically means the fund is run well and the investments made wisely, and vice versa. But caution is needed here: partly because what happened to the units in the past may have little relation to what is going to happen in the future (the fund manager may go for another job, or the particular companies they invest in may be hit by a change in the market), and partly because this measurement is against a continually shifting average. A trust which records an 8% rise in share value may underperform the average one year, the next the average may drop, and the same 8% rise may outperform the average. Magazines such as *Money Management* compare the financial performance of unit trusts on a regular basis.

There are a number of problems with these ethical funds. The fund managers are generally keen to show that their ethical standards are high but that they don't exclude so many companies that the return is adversely affected. As a rough benchmark these trusts invest in some 40% of the companies listed on the Stock Exchange: that is, they regard the other 60% as not being of a suitable ethical standard.

There are hundreds of unit trusts on offer, of which about 40 use ethical criteria. However these criteria can vary considerably.

The ethical criteria used

Some trusts will list the sectors they won't touch and place their investments accordingly. Other funds will place their money in companies which are trying to reduce their harmful activities, and use the investment as a lever to persuade the directors to adopt higher standards. Others will invest in firms offering environmental services such as recycling and waste treatment – these need to be treated with particular caution since many waste companies extol their green credentials but gloss over their poor pollution record and play down their role in merely moving waste around. A full breakdown of the criteria applied by the funds is given in Appendix 2, and you should remember that the standards applied by a given fund may have improved (or worsened) between the writing of this book and the date at which you read it. Only by checking a fund's up-to-date literature for yourself can you be sure how your money will be used at the time you invest it.

The funds also adopt differing positions on what to do if a company ceases to qualify – perhaps because a new subsidiary undertaking an unacceptable activity has been bought. Some funds will sell the shares immediately, others say they will sell as long as the strength of the unit price isn't adversely affected.

There is no standard way of stating the ethical criteria adopted, and there is also no independent auditing of whether the actual investments made meet the criteria the fund states it adopts.

The only ethical criterion adopted by the Fidelity UK Growth Trust, for example, is to exclude shares of 'tobacco or tobacco related companies'.

Conversely, the Global Care Unit Trust from NPI excludes companies involved in the nuclear industry, armaments, tobacco, mining, oil, chemicals, car manufacture and other 'contentious industries' and they generally exclude those involved in using animals for testing products. The fund also actively seeks out companies producing a 'direct social and environmental benefit'. They examine companies' records on staff training, workplace safety, employee relations, environmental and social audits, maternity and paternity leave, eco-labelling and community involvement. They also seek out companies working in the fields of energy conservation, environmental consultancy, public transport, pollution control, recycling, renewable energy and water management. Some of their money is placed with social banks such as Triodos (see Chapter 8) which lends to projects of social and environmental worth.

The Jupiter Ecology Fund has similarly extensive criteria: alcohol, armaments, gambling, nuclear power, pornography, tobacco, animal testing, the uniformity of workers' rights and environmental standards across subsidiaries in different countries, equal opportunities, pollutants, waste, packaging and labelling are all considered before shares are bought.

While some funds will bar investment in companies with any involvement in an 'unacceptable' activity, other trusts will set limits. So the Credit Suisse Fellowship Trust will not invest in 'producers of tobacco or tobacco products and companies which derive more than 10% of their reported annual turnover from the sale of tobacco and tobacco related products'. They also won't invest in 'companies which have received approval from the Ministry of Agriculture, Fisheries and Food, or the Health and Safety Executive to market pesticide products in the UK which include active ingredients that are banned or restricted in five or more countries'. The 10% (which also applies to alcohol) allows Credit Suisse to invest in several supermarkets which sell tobacco and alcohol products. Investors might ask why five countries, and what does 'restricted' mean?

The Jupiter Ecology Fund adopts a lower percentage on tobacco – avoiding investments in companies with more than 1% of turnover from this work. But the 1% also applies to involvement with nuclear and arms companies.

Companies involved in any tobacco or alcohol production are also excluded by the Friends Provident Stewardship Fund, but they go a step further and also bar those involved in the 'distribution of such products where this is a major part of their business'.

The policy adopted on investment in companies using animals also varies widely. The Abbey Life Ethical Trust won't place its funds with companies involved in 'animal experimentation for cosmetics' or 'exploitation of endangered species'. The Equitable Ethical Trust, however, 'will strive to avoid' investments in companies 'involved' in 'animal testing (including drug development)' and the fur trade. In their literature, The Scottish Equitable Ethical Fund is more explicit: 'Any company which conducts any kind of experiments on animals or which manufactures or sells animal tested cosmetics or pharmaceuticals' or any company which sells animal fur products, or 'any company which has any involvement in the production, processing, or sale of meat and poultry products' are 'not currently considered suitable for ethical investment'. This statement is quite clear – except for the inclusion of the word 'currently'. The company says it uses the word as it allows them to change the criteria in the light of customer feedback.

Complying with the criteria in practice

The stated criteria are but one aspect of the funds' ethical practice. The next consideration for any ethical investor is, how are the criteria observed in practice? A note of caution needs to made here, for the funds are constantly buying and selling shares, and the portfolio thus changes month by month. Furthermore the activities of the companies themselves change frequently, so, for example, the acquisition or sale of a subsidiary can move a company from the acceptable to the unacceptable list, or vice versa. It is also a matter of opinion whether particular lines of work are ethical or not.

The nature of large modern companies and the stock market means it is inevitable that it is a matter of opinion whether some investments should or should not have been made by funds.

The Amity Fund, for example says it invests in companies 'which demonstrate a positive contribution to the quality of individual and community life and which respect and protect the environment'.

But Amity has held investments in Glaxo (involved in animal testing) and Northern Foods (whose subsidiary Mayhew Chickens produce battery farmed hens), Kwik-Fit Holdings (part of the motor industry and its contribution to global warming), and various supermarkets (out of town shopping which encourages car use and the decline of local shopping centres).

The Abtrust Ethical Fund seeks companies which make 'a positive contribution to the environment' but nevertheless invested in Powergen in 1995. Powergen was the target of a campaign by Greenpeace who stated the company 'intend to build polluting power stations in Asia which would not meet UK environmental standards, and would threaten to exacerbate air pollution in India and China'; and that they 'have profited directly from delays in the implementation of international acid rain agreements at the expense of wildlife habitats in the UK and Scandinavia'. Greenpeace warned investors that 'the cost of environmental damage resulting from National Power and Powergen's activities outweighs their pre-tax profits ... Don't buy into pollution profits, don't buy shares in ... Powergen'.

Powergen is a well-known company, and many investors looking through the lists of companies the funds invest in are likely to recognise it. Many companies are less well known. For example, the Abtrust and Amity Funds and the Credit Suisse Fellowship Trust (seeking to invest in 'companies which benefit the communities in which they operate') all put money into the company Provident Financial. This company lends money to many people on below-average earnings who repay the loans to weekly doorstep collectors. They thus lend to people who would find it difficult to obtain cheaper credit elsewhere – but with repayments equal to interest rates as high as 100 per cent a year. The company agree their interest rates are 'high compared to rates available from high street banks' but justify them on the basis of 'the cost of the high level of service' of weekly collections.

A popular company for many of these trusts is British Gas whose output is estimated to be contributing 16% of the UK's greenhouse gases, and which was wracked by controversy in 1995 and again in 1996 over the size of salaries, pensions and share options it granted to its senior executives. While there was uproar about the size of the payments, they were only agreed at the shareholders' meeting because the institutional managers either directly voted for them, or, by not registering to vote, allowed the company to act as proxies and vote the increases through. Not only did the managers of the mainstream funds not vote on the issue, it is believed that only a couple of the ethical funds actually voted for the resolution questioning the rises.

(Whether to invest in British Gas raises another ethical question: is it consistent to refuse to invest in British Gas when the likelihood is that you're one of their *customers* anyway?)

Many of the funds invest in supermarket chains. The Jupiter Ecology Fund, Credit Suisse Fellowship Trust, and The Amity Fund have all held shares in Tesco. Apart from concerns about supermarkets encouraging car use by concentrating on out of town sites and transporting food over long

A spoof share certificate produced by Greenpeace to publicise its estimate of the environmental cost of Powergen's activities

distances before sale, Tesco has attracted criticism from Greenpeace. The pressure group has been campaigning to persuade supermarkets to adopt freezer coolants known as 'greenfreeze' which use neither greenhouse gases nor ozone depleting chemicals. Many supermarkets have been adopting the new technology, but Tesco said to Greenpeace in mid 1995: 'Your policy of advocating 'greenfreeze' technology is misguided and, in fact, more environmentally damaging than the alternatives we are pursuing'.

The chemical company Shanks and McEwan has had shares owned by The Amity Fund and The Ethical Trust. Shanks is the parent company of ReChem International which is a leading company in the controversial trade of importing hazardous waste. ReChem incinerates the waste, and land adjacent to one of its sites at Pontypool has been found in a study sponsored by the Welsh Office to have high deposits of dioxins and PCBs. When Environment Minister Robert Atkin announced he was considering prohibiting the import of toxic waste, ReChem responded with a lobbying campaign which was followed by a number of exceptions to the ban.

The company Stagecoach Holdings throws up another difficult question for investors. Shares in this company are held by, among others, the Abtrust Ethical Fund. Investors who are concerned about the environmental impact of private motoring might want to support a bus company such as Stagecoach. However this company has lost six cases after being investigated twenty times for anti-competitive practices by the Monopolies and Mergers Commission. In one judgement against a Stagecoach subsidiary, the Commission described the company's tactics as 'predatory, deplorable and against the public interest'.

Greenpeace's 'Fiasco' lorry on tour in 1994/5, highlighting Tesco's failure to convert its supermarkets to 'greenfreeze'.

By giving these examples of where funds are investing, we are not saying these particular funds are the worst of the bunch, or that they are seeking to mislead investors: merely that there are some difficult decisions to be made.

Charles Jacob, a member of the Committee of Reference (see below) of Friends Provident Stewardship, the largest and oldest ethical fund, cites a company which was on the Ministry of Defence approved contractors list and which therefore should not figure in a fund aimed at people who wished to exclude armaments companies from their portfolio. But closer examination revealed this to be because one of its subsidiaries had supplied one shredding machine for use on HMS Hermes. Part of the military-industrial complex or not?

The funds' operating methods

The trusts adopt very different ways of operating. Henderson Touche Remnant consults holders of its Ethical Fund to find their views on where to invest. One HTR newsletter asks investors 'Given the fact that nuclear power generation has zero emission [sic] compared with gas or coal based power, should the Fund invest in companies involved in nuclear waste management? Or does the long-term nature of radioactive waste and the cost of decommissioning justify the Fund's non-involvement?'

The Family Assurance Friendly Society quietly blazed a new trail in 1996 when it became the first institution to introduce ethical criteria to an existing unit trust. When the Society consulted holders of its United Charities Fund, 98% supported the introduction of ethical criteria, so the fund sold its shares in a wide range of companies, including Rio Tinto Zinc. Regrettably the fund manager did not tell companies why the shares were being sold, but the move should act as a spur to other fund managers to 'go ethical' and to existing unitholders to lobby for the change.

As the world of ethical funds has matured, fund managers have grappled with these ethical questions. In the process, some funds have closed down, among them an environmental fund run by Merchant Investors Insurance. Manager Christopher Jones said they started their Environmental Fund because their sales force said there was customer demand for it. 'I was never very happy about these funds,' said Jones. 'A fund manager has to add value for their clients, and trying to make money on the investments is difficult enough as it is! We didn't have enough policyholders, and I can't claim we had expertise in this area. How can you say one company is more environmentally sound than another? We obviously want a clean environment but from a professional point of view it is much more difficult to take it into account'. (However, Merchant Investors are having another attempt and introduced an Ethical Fund in late 1995. It has a different set of criteria and structure and is being managed by the ethical stockbrokers A.E. Sharp & Co.)

The huge size of companies and trusts means it is very difficult indeed to make informed ethical decisions. The trusts list the companies they invest in as part of their six monthly report – yet prospective investors who inquire may only be given the prospectus which sets out in glowing terms the high standard of living they will attain when they cash in their investments.

Active funds or passive funds?

The National Provident Institution (NPI) is one of the country's oldest and largest financial savings institutions. It offers a wide range of financial products including ethical unit trusts and pensions. It is also one of the few that employs its own research department to brief fund managers on the environmental performance of companies. NPI achieved a small coup with their research department in 1994 when the team working for a rival institution walked out because they believed their work was not being taken seriously enough. They were taken on en bloc by NPI, and now see themselves as a beacon of light in the city.

NPI researcher Mark Campanale says:

'Over the last 20 years, share ownership of companies has become concentrated into the hands of a small number of large and very powerful financial institutions. The corporate culture which thus evolved now reflects the narrow financial interests of these institutions, namely to maximise short term returns. Consequently we have a complete dislocation between the needs of ordinary people and the operation of the national economy. Modern companies squeeze as much profit as they can from the planet's natural resources or pay workers less, so shareholders can be paid more.

'We won't get real change until the values of the fund managers shift more into line with those on whose behalf they invest. There is no doubt that the top 100 financial institutions can have considerable influence over the companies in which they invest.

'The key question is, what is the relationship between these institutions and the management of the companies in which they invest? Do the fund managers use their influence and power to persuade the companies to be more socially responsible? Perhaps all of us involved in managing ethical funds can make a change here. By not just asking detailed questions of management, but also going back to our own investors and communicating to them why particular companies have been chosen. In time we hope to see a rebirth of the traditions of mutuality and self support among investors in the institutions'.

There is no doubt that such a forthright approach is having a knock-on effect on their rivals, at least two of whom are watching NPI closely and are examining their own operating methods.

NPI's approach is to build a rapport with a company, perhaps by meeting with the financial director, visiting a factory and meeting technical staff, and asking them to answer a questionnaire. 'Our hope,' says Campanale, 'is that over time, the responsible investor approach will become the norm. Companies will be forced to become more accountable to the community. That when a fund manager meets a company's directors, questions covering their social and environmental record will be as common as questions on financial matters'.

He advises investors seeking an ethical fund to ask three questions: (1) Are the fund managers active or passive investors, that is, do they raise social issues with companies directly? (2) Do they employ a broad range of disciplines to conduct research, such as social or environmental scientists? (3) Do they publish analytical data on each company included in the portfolio indicating their social or ecological performance?

Other ethical issues

All funds also gloss over another major ethical drawback: that *the funds themselves* are part of large institutions which run other funds which make no claim to invest with ethical criteria in mind. Most people who screen out investments do so because one part of a company indulges in practices perceived to be unacceptable. But where is the logic of then investing in an ethical fund run by a large institution which operates other funds which invest in many companies you would find unacceptable?

The oldest and largest ethical funds are the Stewardship unit trusts run by Friends Provident. Friends introduced the ethical fund and now offer several varieties. But while they 'seek to invest in companies which make a positive contribution to society and avoid those which harm the world or its people,' the policies of the non-ethical funds in the Friends stable are of course very different. In mid 1995, their UK Focus Trust, for example, held shares in Rio Tinto Zinc, British Aerospace, Vickers, Fisons, Glaxo, British American Tobacco, Shell and Forte – companies which have been criticised for their environmental and/or ethical record. Most of the ethical trusts have similar bedfellows – though the fund managers defend this by saying that there simply aren't enough ethical companies on the Stock Exchange to soak up the huge sums they have to invest.

Even worse for some investors is the fact that some institutions running ethical funds are *owned* by companies they would view as unacceptable: the Environmental Opportunities Trust is run by Eagle Star which is owned by British American Tobacco, one of the world's largest cigarette manufacturers.

This is not just of academic importance. There are two main motivations for investing ethically: to ensure money placed is in accordance with the owners' conscience, and to bring pressure to bear on less ethical companies to change their ways. The latter will only happen if the directors believe that they will find it increasingly difficult to gain investment funds because their poor environmental or ethical standards are driving away investors.

Finally, you may wish to consider who *owns* (and *profits from*) the company you invest through. The Ecclesiastical Insurance Group (of which Allchurches Investment and the Amity Fund are a part) is owned by a trust which pays part of its profits to 'the Church of England and other good causes' – a total of £8.8m in the five years to 1995. The United Charities Ethical Trust covenants some of its profits to five national charities (listed on page 153), and donates the commission normally given to financial advisers to the charities.

The best there is

'There's no such thing as ethical investment'. So says John Jones (not his real name), a director of one of the UK's medium sized mainstream funds. Jones' job is to invest £7b, a sum greater than the output of many countries, and the topsy turvy world of finance is well illustrated by the extent of his geographical region. He is responsible for investing in 'Europe' and in his company's eyes that includes from the Arctic in the north to South Africa in the south, and the West Indies in the west to Kashmir in the east!

Even though he is on his company's main board, he does not dare to actively champion the idea of taking ethics into account in his company's investment decisions, for he says that his colleagues – and he heads a team of 400 – would seek to have him sacked. 'Most of the people in my firm don't give a fish's tit about ethics,' he says colourfully. 'People look to us to give them the best returns, and we are duty bound to exercise a fiduciary duty to do that unless the customer limits us. The lead has to come from the investor and not the funds themselves'.

Jones points out that the ethical funds have only attracted a 'tiny' amount of investment. But while he has doubts about ethical issues, he recognises the need to take environmental issues into account. 'Even the most hard-nosed investor who doesn't give a tit for your ethical views will have to accept that they will have to change the way they value investments because of environmental concerns. When we look at evaluating a motor company, or oil or chemicals, arms, waste disposal and power generating firms, we have to follow a line of analysis which says 'environmental impact'. When I first started working that didn't rank at all. You see, deep down many directors of firms believe you (Greens) might be right'.

Some comfort here from the conventional investment world that the dangers of environmental destruction are being realised. But the assessment is still purely on the basis of the financial cost of such destruction and if you want to invest in unit trusts and you believe the ethical funds aren't worth the candle, this is the best you're likely to get from the universe of mainstream money.

The ethical funds may not be perfect, but if you want your money to go into the Stock Exchange, they're the best there is.

How funds influence companies

Some ethical funds do meet with companies to pressurise them to make changes to their business, but such discussions can only really be effective if they can end with the fund managers threatening not to invest, or to sell existing shares, if the company refuses to make changes. If the directors know that the fund will still be putting (sizeable) 'non-ethical' fund money into the company, such discussions and pressure become less effective.

The importance of fund managers and investors meeting directly with companies is not to be underestimated. Individuals wishing to influence a company have the choice of asking questions at the AGM, or writing to the 'customer care' department or similar. The financial institutions have the clout to seek face to face meetings with senior directors.

A survey in 1993 by a University of London researcher, Nicholas Schoenberger, of the small number of ethical fund managers revealed that ten believed they had influence over the companies they invested in, while four didn't, but only four actually had any 'regular' written dialogue with companies on environmental issues, and only five had apparently ever written to a company on the subject. Ten believed in the principle of encouraging companies to become 'better corporate citizens'. The message is that most ethical funds believe they have an influence on companies but have little evidence to base these beliefs on.

Some might ask why fund managers should become directly involved in influencing directors. The reason is that it is the investors in the institutions which own most of the companies through their shareholdings, and the fund managers have a duty to look after what their investors own. According to one analyst, 'if you own a large country house and appoint a manager, you wouldn't expect them to raid the wine cellar, rip up the ornamental gardens, and turn the front room into a brothel. The owner would fire the manager. There is a responsibility to ensure the corporations are managed in a socially-responsible way'.

Furthermore, it is crucial that companies know why funds invest in them or not. If the companies have little idea why a fund isn't buying their shares, they could believe it is because their shares aren't performing well enough – and they need to market their unacceptable products with more determination and flair!

How the funds conduct their research

Most funds rely on screening by EIRIS (see Chapter 6) for information about companies, but some – such as the ethical ones run by NPI, Jupiter Ecology, Allchurches' Amity Fund and Henderson Touche Remnant – have their own departments researching ethical and environmental issues. The NPI research team is headed by Tessa Tennant who also chairs the Social Investment Forum which is trying to encourage ethical investment. The Jupiter Environmental Research Unit includes researchers with backgrounds in both the worlds of finance and environmental pressure groups.

Some funds seek to separate the financial decisions from the ethical. They do this by setting up committees of the 'Green and the Good' from the environmental and ethical world who decide on the ethical criteria and which companies comply. The fund manager – who is the *financial* expert – then selects from this list on the basis of the companies' performance. The membership of such committees is usually detailed in the prospectuses, but they meet in private and there is little independent information telling how effective or rigorous they are. They are also usually appointed by the fund managers rather than the unit holders. A request to Friends Provident for permission to observe a meeting of their Committee was refused on the grounds that the subject of the discussions is their 'intellectual property' and they don't want other funds to know their methods as 'there is still a lot of business to be got out there'.

Although most of the fund managers say they listen carefully to the views of their unitholders, most give little information about the companies in which they invest. NPI, Henderson Touche Remnant and Jupiter Ecology all publish newsletters giving background information on the companies whose shares they own, and decisions made on buying and selling. The TSB Environmental Investor Fund uses their six monthly manager's report to describe the companies and give the main reason for buying the shares.

Only a few of the funds hold meetings of the unitholders, among them the CIS Environ Fund, the Friends Provident Ethical Investment Trust, and the Jupiter International Green Investment Trust.

Assessing performance

Trying to decide which fund is providing the best performance is rather like entering a minefield. The institutions running unit trusts release numerous graphs and percentages telling how well their investments are doing, but the bottom line is that their future performance is simply unpredictable.

The statutory warning funds include on their literature, that previous performance is not a guide to what may happen in the future, should be taken seriously – except that there is little else the investor can use to make a judgement apart from past performance. In theory interviewing the fund managers about how they work should help you to make up your mind if this is a fund you want to buy into, but in practice few have the expertise to ask the searching questions necessary, and in any case most fund managers would not be keen to meet prospective investors on this basis.

Past performance is given for unit trusts based on percentage increases, and their ranking according to other funds. A high percentage increase *may* show the fund has been well managed, but closer examination is needed. A 100% rise over five years may look favourable, but a large proportion of the increase may have come from a handful of investments which performed well at a particular time (if, for example, some takeover bids increased the price of the target company's shares), and the rest of the time the performance may have been quite lacklustre.

Also, percentage increases need to be compared to some sort of base line. The notorious swindler Bernard Cornfeld who ran unit trusts in the 1960s trumpeted the large percentage increases his funds had experienced since a particular year. But he persistently omitted the history of his funds in the two previous years – they crashed just after he launched them. Cornfeld expressed the 'rises' from this bottom figure, which was of course far lower than the original issue price, thereby purportedly showing a higher percentage growth.

Performance over time can also vary for ordinary human reasons connected with who is managing a fund. The performance analysts Allenbridge Group PLC cite the example of the Credit Suisse Fellowship Fund. They say: 'Since William Mott and Stephanie Howard took over the management of this fund in September 1993, performance has strengthened considerably and it is one of the top overall performers in the UK Growth Sector. In the period since 1987 the fund had an annualised growth of only 9 per cent, the lowest in the sector. In contrast, when looking at performance since September 1993, the fund's annualised growth has more than doubled to 19.19 per cent and is 9 per cent above the sector average'. Hence some confidence can be expressed in Mott and Howard, but there is no guarantee how long they will stay as managers of the fund.

Another ethical fund showed good performance – until the fund manager went on maternity leave and her colleagues were left to hold the fort. While the manager had her baby the fund performed less well, and then within weeks of her return the performance had perked up.

In essence performance is as much a matter of comparison with other similar funds as a question of whether it is high or low. When assessing which fund to buy into, draw up a table of their performances as they are when you intend to invest. This can be done based on the ratings published by magazines such as *Money Management*. The table should show the performance of the ethical funds relative to each other, and relative to the non-ethical funds.

Such table could include:

• The type of fund: whether profits are paid in cash to provide income, or by the issuing of more units to produce a growth in the capital; whether the fund only invests in the UK or further afield; and whether it is a unit trust or an investment trust (see below).

• The percentage rise over the previous year and the previous five years.

• The percentage rise of the FT-SE Index – the average of all the companies listed on the Stock Exchange.

• The ranking of the fund compared to all (ethical and non-ethical) funds of the same type, expressed as, say, third highest performance of 143 funds.

The chart overleaf compares performances at March 1996.

In reaching your decision, it is also worth listening to the views of the financial advisers (see Chapter 10) who should have had some contact with the funds and be able to express an opinion on which is being well managed.

A fund of funds

Many investors believe that placing their money in a unit trust will provide a sufficient spread of companies to reduce the financial risk to an acceptable degree. But in the world of finance people are always seeking 'more'. It was in response to such cries that the fund of funds were born.

The funds compared

Fund type	Fund name	% rise in 1 yr	FT-SE rise in 1 yr	Rank in 1 yr	% rise in 5 yrs	FT-SE rise in 5 yrs	Rank in 5 yrs
UK Growth & Income	Scot Amicable Equity Income	15.1%	27.2%	103/106	65.2%	87.3%	50/118
UK Growth	Allchurches Amity	17.5%	27.2%	101/143	52.8%	87.3%	106/121
	Credit Suisse Fellowship	37.5%	27.2%	2/143	n/a		n/a
	Eagle Star Env'tal Opportunities	15.9%	27.2%	118/143	78.4%	87.3%	38/121
	Friends Provident Stewardship	25.1%	27.2%	55/143	80.9%	87.3%	35/121
	Scottish Equitable Ethical	21.9%	27.2%	51/143	67.5%	87.3%	58/121
	Sovereign Ethical	36.1%	27.2%	7/143	65.6%	87.3%	65/121
	TSB Environmental Investor	15.9%	27.2%	117/143	62.2%	87.3%	80/121
UK Equity Income	Friends Provident Stewardship Inc	11.6%	27.2%	66/84	71.1%	87.3%	22/74
International Growth	Abtrust Ethical	22.4%	27.2%	38/176	n/a		n/a
	CIS Environ Trust	16.7%	27.2%	104/176	91.8%	87.3%	40/125
	City Financial Acorn Ethical	12.9%	27.2%	139/176	73.3%	87.3%	81/125
	Clerical Medical Evergreen	5.2%	27.2%	172/176	35%	87.3%	124/125
	Equitable Ethical	14.0%	27.2%	131/176	n/a		n/a
	Framlington Health	93.8%	27.2%	1/176	284.7%	87.3%	2/125
	HTR Ethical	18.4%	27.2%	76/176	n/a		n/a
	Jupiter Ecology Fund	23.9%	27.2%	26/176	86.0%	87.3%	48/125
	NPI Global Care	23.9%	27.2%	27/176	n/a		n/a

NOTE: All funds are compared with other funds of the same type to take into account the different risks.

The percentage rises take into account the difference between the price at which the fund managers will sell units and the price at which they will buy them back.

The rises over 1 and 5 years are for the periods ending in March 1996.

The rankings compare the funds with all (ethical and non-ethical) funds of the same type: thus 50/118 means the fund was 50th highest out of 118 funds.

Where n/a is indicated, the funds in question had not been operating for 5 years.

These are unit trust funds which don't invest in companies directly, but use the money placed with them by investors to buy a range of units in other unit trusts, company and government bonds, and perhaps other financial vehicles. The thinking is that such buying spreads the risk further as investors are not exposed to a potentially poor performance by one particular fund.

There are ethical funds of funds, but a major drawback for investors is that they have to look at an even wider range of funds and companies to decide if the particular companies in each fund all meet their ethical criteria.

Furthermore, there is another layer of fees payable to the financial inter-mediaries running the fund. Also, some of these funds are run by the independent financial advisers (see Chapter 10) which could cause conflicts of interest if they recommend their own funds in preference to others.

Two such funds are run by the financial advisers Barchester Green Investment. Their Green Ethical Unit Trust Portfolio and Minerva Green Ethical Portfolio invests in other funds which, they consider, take ethical issues seriously.

Pensions

For many people, pensions are the second largest item of expenditure they will make: first comes the house purchase, second comes the pension, and third comes the car. (Strictly speaking, there's a fourth area of expenditure which consumes even more money than the pension, but it would seem churlish to include the cost of bringing up a child in the same list as a car or house). Yet the information provided about pensions rarely allows savers to decide whether it might be better to use their money differently.

Pensions are sold on the basis that they will provide you with an income after you retire. The investor contracts to pay a set sum every month to the pension company, which generally invests the money in its unit trust. When the saver comes to retirement age, some – usually a quarter – of the accrued sum can be withdrawn, and the remainder is used to buy what is termed an 'annuity'. In return for the remaining lump sum being handed over, the annuity company agrees to pay out a certain sum every month until the recipient dies – however long that is. This sum is the pension you will receive. The annuity has to be bought within a fixed period after the date you say you are retiring – whatever the state of the stock market or the annuity market at the time (the return on annuities varies from time to time according to a number of complex financial issues).

The crucial issue is that pensions are long term savings plans where you enter into a legal contract to continue to deposit stated sums – and if you later want to vary the arrangement you are, in effect, begging the pension company to allow you to breach the contract.

Pensions are set up with a variety of mechanisms. With some the investor pays the same amount every month until they retire; with others the saver agrees to pay a premium which rises each year in line with inflation. Some pensions will pay out a monthly sum specified in advance, while others will pay out according to how the stock market performs. Each year the pension fund may declare bonuses which are added to the sums accrued so far.

People investing in a pension plan which does not specify how much will actually be paid out can suffer from the year by year whims of the stock market. If you happen to retire when the market has crashed (and these occasions are not that rare) your lump sum will be far less than if you had perhaps retired a few months or even days earlier when the market was booming.

From the point of view of the financial institutions, pensions can be a golden egg. Once the customer has signed on the dotted line, the money comes in, usually by direct debit, every month, for twenty or thirty years, regular as clockwork. The buyers of many pension plans enter into these agreements often without any undertaking by the pension company as to exactly how they will perform, how much pension will eventually be paid, and, in the case of ethical pension plans, whether the ethical standards will change during the plan's existence.

All this makes it difficult if not impossible to work out exactly what your pension will be, or even whether you are receiving the right amount when you do retire. It's fair to say that pensions are probably the most complicated area of the financial world accessible to the individual investor, and even many financial advisers (see Chapter 10) find it difficult to keep up to date and understand all the nuances of individual plans. The literature from the companies offering pensions is rarely written in an easily comprehensible form.

The tax advantages

Pensions have been marketed aggressively in the last twenty years with a principal selling point being the tax benefit. The government has wanted to reduce the number of people reliant on state pensions, so it has offered tax advantages on pension plans. In broad terms this involves a rebate of income tax paid on the monthly contributions, although income tax is payable when the pension is eventually paid out. Thus if you are on the basic rate of income tax at 24%, for every £100 you earn, £24 will be deducted by the Inland Revenue. But if you pay that remaining £76 into a pension plan, the Revenue will reimburse the £24 which also goes to the pension fund on your behalf. The funds are also not required to pay tax on their investment profits, in theory allowing for some of those profits to be added to the sums available to their customers.

Financial plans which rely for their worth on particular tax regimes need to be treated cautiously – especially ones spread over many years. A change of government might mean that the tax benefits from pension plans could be swept away, or just left to wither on the vine. A taste of this was given in late 1995 when the government announced it was reducing the basic rate of income tax – a knock-on effect being that less money will be credited by the Inland Revenue to pension plans.

Charges

Only since the beginning of 1995 have the various financial companies and intermediaries who set up the plans had to declare their charges: and the sums make depressing reading. On the one hand they can be a high percentage of the amounts paid into the fund, and on the other they can be levied in a highly complicated and seemingly illogical way according to how long the customer has been paying the premiums, and how long it is until they retire.

Plain English?

The fees investors are charged for pension plans are contained in the small print, rather than the glossy pictures at the front of the brochures. Skandia Life, which offers ethical pensions, tells prospective purchasers the following about its fees:

- Allocation to units at a minimum level of 100%.
- 5% bid/offer spread (plus rounding adjustment of up to 1%) applied only to regular contributions.
- 1%pa Establishment Charge applied only to single contributions, transfer payments and any DSS contributions (in respect of contracting-out) for the five years following allocation.
- Loyalty bonus of up to 6% when benefits become payable in respect of single contributions, transfer payments and DSS contributions invested for six years or more.
- $3/4$% Annual Management Charge. (Skandia Life reserves the right to increase this charge in the future.)
- Competitive Maintenance Charge, currently $2.35 per month, deducted from value of the fund. (Skandia Life reserves the right to increase this charge in the future.)
- Annual charges for fund management reflect the nature of the underlying assets and the degree of external management of the fund(s) chosen.
- Other charges depend on individual plan circumstances, e.g. Contribution Servicing Charge, Early Encashment Charge, charge for early encashment of investment in a Secure Performance Plus Fund.

Is that clear?

In some cases as much as one third of the total amount paid into a pension plan can be deducted in charges. So if you pay in £25,000 over 25 years (£1000 a year), about £8,000 of that could be paid out in fees and won't be invested on your behalf at all.

To add to the confusion, the charges have to be quoted to the customer at the outset based on the size of the premiums paid, while the actual calculation of what is charged year by year is based mainly on how much the investments in the fund are earning. Hence the charges could be higher than the figures quoted at the outset if the fund performs well, and lower if it performs badly.

The pension plans use a variety of mechanisms for withdrawing their commission fees. Many use the method known as 'front-end loading' which involves most of the fees being paid out from the contributions made during the first few years. So much of your early years' payments may not be invested on your behalf at all: they may go towards paying charges. Other pension companies take their fees spread through later years, thus giving more time for the early repayments to be invested and earning profit.

There are more serious implications with front end loading if the buyer doesn't stay the course. If you want to back out of the plan (perhaps you become dissatisfied with the financial acumen of the fund managers, or they change their ethical criteria – which generally aren't part of the contract – or perhaps you lose your job and can't afford the payments), when you cancel the plan you may not get back all that you have paid in, let alone any profits that could have been earnt.

A 30 year pension plan quoted by one company where £100 is credited to the pension plan every month (£75 plus £25 tax rebate) shows payments in, charges extracted, and value of the pension (how much you will receive if you withdraw from the plan, and assuming the investments have grown at 9% a year) as follows:

Year	Total paid in to date	Total charges to date	Value of fund
1	£1,200	£719	£538
5	£6,000	£2,040	£4,910
10	£12,000	£3,410	£13,400
15	£18,000	£5,360	£25,900
20	£24,000	£7,880	£44,400
22	£26,400	£9,220	£54,000
25	£30,000	£3,410	£80,300
26	£31,200	£1,950	£90,200
30	£36,000	£3,050	£131,000

Thus the company levies a total of over £9,000 in charges if you are a customer for 22 years. If, however, you remain a customer for another four years, they only charge a total of just under £2,000. If you stayed the course for 30 years, the total charges would be £3,200.

The financial industry defends these charges on the basis that if you've paid in £36,000 and the pension fund has invested it to produce £131,000, then fees of £3,050 is good value for money – but that's if you stay the course and the investments produce 9% a year.

These peculiar arrangements come about because the companies refund fees charged in earlier years to customers who remain for the entire length of the contract. But the structure also means that with this plan, the customer has to be paying in for nearly 10 years before there is any benefit at all: £12,000 paid in, and the fund worth only £13,400 (again assuming the investments grow at 9% a year).

The fees levied can also vary if the investor decides to increase their contributions. Some companies will charge much higher fees if you increase your monthly payment than if you pay the same amount as an occasional lump sum in addition to the premiums hitherto agreed. In other words, if you want to pay an extra £600 a year into your pension fund, it may be worthwhile making annual single payments of that sum rather than increasing your monthly payment by £50.

The lesson from endowment mortgages

In mid 1994 endowment mortgages were the centre of a scandal for two reasons: firstly many people were found to want to back out of them in the first few years, and therefore lost sizeable sums because fees are 'front-end loaded' in the same way as many pensions. Secondly the stock market was found to be underperforming and some investments were not making sufficient return to pay off the mortgages. Pension plans work in a similar way to endowment mortgages in that they are long term and the hope is that the investments will produce a profit, yet there is little sign that the lesson learnt from the endowment scandal has been applied to pensions.

The justification for all these high and complicated fees is rather obscure, and one can't help coming to the conclusion that the pension funds believe that since the buyer gets generous tax rebates on their contributions, the companies might as well share in the bonanza.

Financial advisers are keen to point out that pensions shouldn't be bought on the basis of which company is charging the lowest fees, but which company is making the wisest investments. Investors who believe that if you pay peanuts, you get monkeys, might plump for a fund charging high fees. Other savers might feel that a lower charging structure means the fund managers are not so greedy. The professionals involved in setting up pension plans also point out that people selling other products in the marketplace, such as train journeys, baskets of groceries or television sets, are not required to reveal how much they are earning out of the deal so why should the providers of pensions have to declare their earnings? But when buying groceries, televisions or what-have-you, the buyer knows more or less what they are going to get for their money, while pension institutions often give no undertakings as to what the eventual pension will be.

Inflation

Furthermore, when inflation is taken into account the eventual pension may not seem as attractive as it would appear in the company brochures. An investor paying £50 per month into a pension plan for 20 years can expect an annual pension of £1200 if the stock market grows at 6% a year – but after inflation of 3% a year is taken into account, that £1200 will be equal to about £450 per year at 1996 prices. If the stock market grows by 12%, the annual pension will be nearly £3400, equal to nearly £1300 after inflation. (These deemed 6% and 12% rises in the stock market are those quoted by pension companies according to the various regulations governing such schemes; but ethical investors ought to remember that the government aims at growth in the economy of some 3% a year – a figure not always attained.)

So if you want to receive the level of pension quoted when you first talk to a financial adviser or company, you'll need to be prepared to continually increase your monthly contributions. The pension company is likely to be aware of this, and each year they will try to persuade you to increase your premiums as inflation bites.

These facts and figures put pensions in a different light from the rosy glow painted by many in the financial services industry. And while the pension funds can't predict how the plans will perform financially, they can play even faster and looser with the ethical issues.

The ethical issues

Some of the institutions offering ethical and green unit trusts will link a pension to them: that is, the money paid in for the pension is then put in the ethical unit trust. However the actual pension is usually paid out of the annuity plan which is bought when the person retires – and in 1996 there were actually no ethical annuities available despite the claims by a number of funds that they are selling 'ethical pensions'. (Of course, ethical annuities may be introduced by the time today's pension clients retire.)

Money put in a unit trust can usually be recovered at any time: the running cost is generally the one-off 5% plus 1% per year fees which the manager earns. If the ethical standards change, it is not necessarily that painful to sell the units and switch to another fund. For the investor locked into a pension plan until retirement, it would be all too easy to find money going into companies they disapprove of. For example if the rate of global warming increases dramatically during the term of the pension plan, the fund manager might decide that climate change is more dangerous than the problems posed by nuclear power, and they might begin investing in the nuclear industry – a decision most environmentally minded investors would find abhorrent.

Other investors may object when a fund is bought out or merges with another institution. In mid 1996 Clerical Medical which runs an ethical fund was up for sale, and a front runner was the NatWest Bank, one of the banks at the centre of controversy because of loans to Third World countries.

Since the institutions which offer pensions normally link them with their unit trusts, investors are likely to conclude that their pension premiums are to be invested as though they were buying directly into the unit trust. But caution is needed here, for although by law the fund has to present a twice yearly report to *unit fund holders* detailing exactly where the fund invests, there is no such legal requirement to declare where *pension funds* are invested.

While there are over 40 ethical unit trusts, there are fewer ethical pension plans, and the same criteria need to be applied to the plans as when investing direct in companies or unit trusts.

The responsibilities of fund managers

Since a pension is likely to be the second largest purchase many people will ever make, it follows that pension companies have huge incomes. Indeed it is estimated that over three-quarters of the shares on the Stock Exchange are held by pension funds and insurance companies (which provide pensions as well as insurance cover).

The investment decisions are made by the fund managers acting on behalf of the investors. Thus, while the pension fund managers are not the owners of industrial and commercial Britain, they are the ones who *control* whole swathes of it – and there are not many of them.

Some City observers believe that Britain's major companies are controlled by as few as 15 pension and insurance fund managers: their decisions on whether to invest, attend annual general meetings, and influence the composition of the board of directors, shape the ethos of Britain's largest companies. The prevailing view of these fund managers has been to seek the highest profit with the lowest risk: so if you want ethical considerations taken into account by your pension fund, you have to make that view known.

These problems should not be taken to mean that buying a pension is necessarily unwise: rather that you should consider the following questions very carefully before you buy into a pension plan:

Will you be able to keep up the premiums for many years?

Where is the money to be invested?

What fees are charged and when are they levied?

What is the record of the fund managers?

Then calculate what would be the return if you were to save using a different method such as a PEP (Personal Equity Plan). You also need to ask whether, in practice, you would actually put away the sum every month if it was purely voluntary and you were not locked into a 'compulsory' plan.

There is also that great imponderable of how long you personally are likely to live after retirement. If you are healthy, a pension plan might be a wise move: if you're not, or you're leading an unhealthy life, it may be worth reflecting whether a pension is the best option.

In summary, we all need a way of ensuring an income when we are too old to work: pensions as they are set up at present seem unlikely to provide the income most people are going to want, but there are few alternatives.

Personal Equity Plans (or PEPs)

PEPs evolved because the government wanted to encourage small savers to invest in the stock market. While profits on unit trusts or share dividends attract income and capital gains tax, earnings from PEPs have tax exemptions. The conditions can change each year (as they can with *all* financial plans arranged with tax benefits in mind) and generally stipulate a maximum that can be invested in any one year.

In 1996 individuals could invest via a PEP a maximum of £6,000 per year in a unit trust or investment trust, and a further £3,000 in the shares of a single company. In return, the profits – dividends and any rise in the price of the units or the shares – are paid free of income and capital gains tax. The regulations do not allow you to start more than one PEP in each financial year. The companies offering PEPs will normally accept lump sums or regular monthly payments. PEPs give the investor more flexibility than long term plans such as pensions: money can be paid in or withdrawn at will without high penalties.

The fees for a PEP will normally be the same as those charged for the unit trust it is attached to – the 5% difference between the buying and selling price, plus an annual 1% management charge.

Just as they do for pensions and life assurance, the unit trusts provide the underlying vehicle for PEPs. You need to seek out a PEP which is attached to an ethical unit trust plan, and then examine the ethics of the fund and the companies it invests in as if you were investing directly.

PEPs are available through the Abtrust Ethical Fund, the Acorn Ethical

Unit Trust, the Albert E. Sharp Ethical PEP, Allchurches Amity, CIS Environ, Credit Suisse Fellowship, Eagle Star Environmental Opportunities, Equitable Ethical, Framlington Health, Friends Provident Stewardship, Genesis Life, Henderson Touche Remnant, Jupiter Ecology, NPI Global Care, Scottish Equitable and Sovereign Ethical.

PEPs obviously provide a tax efficient way of investing in the Stock Exchange, although they are not available for investing in non-Stock Exchange listed companies – a discrepancy which puts companies in the social economy (see Chapter 9) at a further disadvantage.

Investment trusts

Unit trusts and investment trusts do the same job of spreading investors' money across many company shares, but in different ways. The difference illustrates the way money is being made out of money with only a loose connection with the profits to be made from providing people with the goods and services they want.

An investment trust is a company listed on the Stock Exchange whose business is investing in the shares of other companies. While a conventional company has assets such as factories and machinery, shops and staff, the assets of an investment trust are the shares it owns in other companies.

Like unit trusts, the investment trusts attract investors because they spread the financial risk across many companies. But while the value of unit trusts only rises and fall as the underlying company shares rise and fall, investment trust shares also rise and fall because they can be sold on to other investors (as opposed to only being sold back to the fund managers, as is the case with unit trusts), and the price of the shares therefore floats according to demand. Like an ordinary company's shares, as demand goes up for the investment trust's shares, the price rises, and vice versa. And this rise and fall depends on the investors expectations of how well the investment trust will perform.

There are a small number of ethical investment trusts: they list their investments in a similar way to unit trusts.

8

Banks and building societies

● ●

'A bank is an organisation which lends you an umbrella when the sun is
shining… and demands it back when it rains'.
Anon.

MOST SMALL INVESTORS and savers have little to do with stocks and
shares, unit trusts and investment trusts, pensions and PEPs: they
simply put their money in a bank or building society.

Banks evolved as businesses that earned their profits by holding and
managing money for individuals and companies. In return for issuing
chequebooks and processing the payment of cheques, the banks would
charge fees, or gain income from lending out money which had been
deposited with them but which was not likely to be immediately wanted. In
today's financial world, banks make less money out of providing services
than they do from investing and lending money directly to huge corporations
or via the international money markets.

Building societies evolved as a way for people to pool their savings in a
non-profit-making institution and buy their own homes.

In the 1990s, the activities of both these segments of the financial world
are causing deep concern to many people who wish their money to be used
for positive good, rather than just for making money.

Many observers believe that the explosion in the range of financial services
being offered has been caused by the banks seeking other ways of earning
money than by lending. The theory is based on the huge losses which the big
banks are facing because of their lending to Third World countries. In the late
1980s countries such as Brazil and Mexico forced the commercial banks to
whom the loans were owing to reschedule the debts. These reschedulings
mean the country perhaps pays a lower interest rate over a longer period,
thus reducing its immediate payments. For the banks, such as the UK 'big
four' – NatWest, Midland, Lloyds, and Barclays – it meant the possibility of
'losing' vast sums and having to demonstrate to shareholders that they were
diversifying, and hence seeking other ways to earn their profits.

This desire to diversify has caused banks to establish a wide range of financial services which only a few years ago we had no idea we needed. At the same time, it has caused them to reduce conventional banking work – which is not so profitable.

Recent years have seen controversy around the issue of 'redlining' whereby mainstream banks simply won't lend to any customer living in particular districts because the area is viewed as being poor and the residents unreliable at paying back loans. Some banks are even trying to discourage the use of money itself so people increasingly use credit and debit cards and the banks can take a bigger cut on the transaction.

Within this maelstrom of financial contracts, ethical investors have been looking very critically at the work of the large banks, and a small clutch of ethical and social banks have opened in response. The principal ethical question to ask of banks is, *Who are they lending money to?* And, in most cases, the answer is: they won't tell you. Confidentiality in banking is seen as sacrosanct, and the conventional banks won't tell you who their customers are.

Large companies themselves however, usually will, and the annual reports of public companies will state which bank they use. Thus Lloyds are the bankers for British American Tobacco (cigarette manufacturers); and all the big four provide services to British Aerospace (the UK's largest defence contractor).

As with all ethical matters, investors will need to decide where to draw the line when choosing or rejecting a bank. The decision is not that easy since most of the banks which provide chequebooks and have sufficient branches to allow regular drawing of cash have been the target of intense criticism. According to the World Development Movement,

> Lloyds, Midland, Barclays and NatWest have lent huge sums of money to Third World governments, many of whose leaders were unelected or corrupt. Each (government) has made sure that the people of the Third World pay the price by borrowing more and more to pay ever increasing interest charges. These are the Piggy Banks. The people of the Third World, in country after country, have successfully overthrown the generals and dictators and embraced democracy. But, saddled with unpayable debt, they are actually poorer now than ten years ago.

Friends of the Earth took this issue a stage further with their campaign to persuade account holders to boycott the big four. According to FoE,

> In the last ten years, the rate of rainforest destruction has virtually doubled as heavily indebted Third World countries have cleared vast areas of rainforest for timber and cash crop cultivation to pay their debts to banks in rich northern countries, including the UK.

FoE estimate that the main UK high street banks are owed £8b by Third World countries, and in 1992 such debts made Lloyds £200m profit, and Midland £171m profit – 96% of the latter's total profit!

The debt trap

Barclays and NatWest were two banks in a consortium which loaned nearly US $12b to the Philippines when President Marcos was in power. It was for a nuclear power station at Morong, Bataan, at the foot of a volcano in the Pacific earthquake zone. *The plant has never functioned* but it still costs the people of the Philippines US$350,000 per day in interest payments. In 1992 the country had a US$27b external debt, including nearly US$800m owed to UK banks.

Building societies are likely to rank higher on the ethical scale, since their main lending is for housing. In theory they are non-profitmaking bodies, that is they are wholly owned by their members. While most of their money is lent to individual homebuyers, they will still place money on the overnight money markets to ensure their funds earn income during the hours after they close each day. They can also lend a small proportion of their funds for non-housing purposes, and like banks, they generally won't reveal who to.

While recent years have seen a huge growth in the number of ethical unit trusts and pensions, this has not been mirrored in the sector where most people put their money: the banks and building societies. Indeed in early 1996 there are only three institutions operating in these areas with ethical policies: the Co-operative and Triodos banks, and the Ecology Building Society. While none of these can provide branches on most high streets, in some instances account holders can use Link cash dispensers or similar facilities at the mainstream banks to draw cash and/or pay in cheques.

With some of the larger building societies now turning themselves into banks, owned no longer by their members but by shareholders and other financial institutions, ethical investors also have to consider the question of *ownership*. The 'mutual' building societies continue to be owned and, in principle, controlled by their members – though when it comes to electing board members, it is very rare indeed for an ordinary member of a society to be elected to its board. The culture of many of the (mutual) building societies is little different from many PLCs — with profit being the watchword, employees having similar working conditions to bank staff, and little personal contact between customer and local manager. However, as an investor in a building society that has opted to become a PLC, you have no control or say whatever in the running of the society or its investment policy (unless you also buy shares and seek to have your say at the AGM – see Chapter 11).

The mutual societies claim they will always be able to pay higher rates of interest because all their 'profit' is distributed as interest to investors, with none of it siphoned off to pay a dividend to shareholders.

Standards – what standards?

'Again NatWest proved that principles came a poor second to cash in the heady world of high street banking'. So said men's magazine *Maxim* after setting up four bogus companies involved in highly dubious businesses in a sting to test the ethical standards of the high street banks.

NatWest welcomed the porn company 'Young and Shaven' as a client after being assured that 'nothing illegal will be going on... I mean, all the girls look sixteen'. Lloyds, the Midland and NatWest gave useful business advice to the entrepreneurs setting up Pipe and Rocks – a magazine for the 'hard-core dealer' – with the former advising that they should set up as a limited company 'in case someone kills themselves with drugs after reading the magazine'.

NatWest and Barclays were willing to have 'The White British Party' as account holders, with the former's small business adviser only looking slightly concerned when told that the treasurer 'had a few criminal convictions'. But the concern passed after learning the convictions were not for financial irregularities. Barclays said 'political parties were fine by them, whatever the beliefs of their members' and only hesitated when asked for a loan for 'office equipment, baseball bats, things like that'.

Even 'Napalm Inc' was offered an account by Lloyds, Barclays and NatWest despite the letterhead which stated 'Tested on Asians, not on Animals'.

The Co-operative Bank (to its credit) refused to take accounts from any of them. When the scam was revealed the spokespeople of the big four banks said they would not do business with people involved in any illegal activities, and that no accounts had actually been opened by the spoof companies.

The Co-operative Bank

This is the only medium sized bank which has actively sought to attract the ethical saver. It launched its ethical stance in 1992 with a tightly drawn list of ethical criteria. It has been an effective marketing strategy, but because banks operate under a duty of confidentiality it is difficult to know whether the Co-op will exactly meet your own individual ethical criteria. This contrasts with unit trusts (see Chapter 7) where the fund managers list the companies they invest in. The Co-op, like most banks, produces no such list of corporate customers, and customers are thus reliant on the broad policies the bank has decided to adopt. Ethical investors will also note that the bank numbers among its subsidiaries the decidedly non-ethical Unity Trust Bank (see page 86).

The Co-operative have made their ethical stance central to their public profile (the ethical stance appears on the cover and opening pages of their annual reports for 1992, '93 and '94). However, taking any ethical stance always invites more questions, particularly since it is so unusual for a bank to consider anything but profit. The Co-op admit they have had an uphill job persuading some that their policy is genuine and not just a marketing ploy. It was drawn up after consulting their half million customers and the bank stresses they are not a campaigning body, but are reflecting their customers' concerns. The issue, according to the bank, is just where to draw the line. Thus their declaration that they will not 'invest in or supply financial services to any regime or organisation which oppresses the human spirit, takes away the rights of individuals, or manufacturers any instrument of torture' begs other questions. For instance, which countries are on the boycott list? Some might ask whether Britain itself is on it, since the pattern of legislation here has progressively taken away the 'rights of individuals'. The bank will not issue a list of countries they boycott, saying they don't want to single these countries out unfairly. They say they deal with requests from prospective customers on a case by case basis, and have turned business away, but they won't list the companies affected.

The difficulty of relying on customers' views is revealed by their policy that the bank will 'not speculate against the pound using either its own money or that of its customers'. This takes the bank away from areas which customers can easily understand – like animal testing, lending to arms companies, and providing services to factory farms – to the more complex area of trading on the money markets. This trading is central to the activities of nearly all banks as in theory they need to even out the daily ebbs and flows of providing and taking in cash. But it does mean that money is routinely loaned to other banks and to companies and the government. The Co-op says that although they won't speculate against the pound on the currency markets, they continue with the 'normal bank trading' on the money markets. This means that Co-op customers' money will be finding its way – eventually – to finance activities account holders could find unacceptable.

The Co-op admits that if customers appreciated the difficult water an ethical bank is led into by such trading, most would oppose it, but explaining the issue to most account holders is not easy, and the Co-op has not tried. The bank also says it would have to consider very carefully the effect of such a decision on its ability to comply with the extensive banking regulations.

Prospective customers going over the Co-op's ethical stance with an eye for detail could legitimately read different meanings into phrases such as 'will not provide banking services', 'will not invest in', 'will not support', and 'will not engage in' when applied to different kinds of business. In fact it seems to be just a question of sloppy phrasing: the bank says the expressions all mean the same, and it won't accept as customers (for example) 'tobacco product manufacturers', anyone who makes or supplies weapons for or to 'any country which has an oppressive regime', cosmetics firms that experiment on animals, anyone 'using exploitative factory farming methods' or 'engaged in the production of animal fur', or 'any organisation involved in blood sports'. In 1996 the bank extended its ethical policy to include a pledge to 'actively seek and support the business of organisations which promote the concept of "Fair Trade"', and to 'welcome suppliers whose activities are compatible with its ethical policy'.

Though we may have reservations, such doubts should not be taken to mean the bank's ethical policy is worthless, but rather that the higher your ethical standards, the more likely it is that you will find the Co-op is using your money (or allowing others to use it) for purposes of which you disapprove. And conversely, the more likely it is you will find the Co-op better than most other banks. The ethical policy has undoubtedly produced customers for the Co-op, and a large number of campaigning and environmental groups in particular have chosen to bank there – but many have been surprised to find they have to pay bank charges as the bank classes them as businesses.

If all banks adopted these ethical polices, many firms involved in unacceptable practices would find it very difficult to obtain banking services.

The Co-operative Bank is also unique among banks in that while legislation forbids a co-operative from becoming a clearing bank (so the Co-op Bank is a PLC, not itself a co-op), it is nonetheless a wholly owned subsidiary of the CWS (Co-operative Wholesale Society), to which it pays its profits by way of a dividend (nearly £10m in 1995). The CWS itself is the central federal organisation of the retail Co-operative movement, and is owned by the local retail Co-op societies themselves. So the more profitable the bank becomes, the more advantageous in turn for your local Co-op.

Triodos Bank

Triodos is probably Britain's most innovative and imaginative bank. It is owned by shareholders, through non-voting shares in a Dutch trust which protects the social and environmental aims of the bank. The trust (Foundation for the Administration of Triodos Bank Shares) holds the sole voting rights in the bank but receives no dividend. It protects Triodos against takeovers or 'untoward influences', and listens to and represents the views of shareholders at the AGM. The bank has branches in the Netherlands, Belgium and (since taking over Mercury Provident) the UK. It will lend money only to projects having social or environmental worth, and has pioneered a number of trailblazing accounts and loan arrangements intended to help individuals, small businesses, charities and organisations in the social economy to raise the money needed for a wide range of useful projects. Its underlying principle is to encourage savers and investors to know exactly to whom their money is to be loaned, and preferably to specify where it is to go. Yet it takes deposits and pays specified interest rates, and in 1996 introduced a current account with chequebooks and a bill paying facility to further expand the services they offer.

Triodos has given loans to the British Organic Farmers and Growers Association, organic farms, wholefood shops, a co-op specialising in sustainable timber, Steiner schools, communities running social development courses, trusts providing workshops for people with special needs, wind energy companies, holistic health clinics, housing associations, a Citizens' Advice Bureau, theatre companies, and companies supporting Third World enterprises.

The bank says it supports only those businesses and projects 'which are socially, ecologically and financially sustainable, which benefit the community, enhance the environment and respect human freedom'. It publishes regular lists of their loans.

In addition to giving conventional loans secured on property, Triodos also runs a number of different schemes to assist projects which can't provide such security. One account allows deposit account holders to target their investment to particular sectors (such as housing, environmental projects, education etc.) or specific projects. Savers can specify the interest they want (within limits) and this reflects the interest charged to the projects the money is lent to. In another scheme 'communities of guarantors' underwrite a loan – so, for instance, parents at a school could individually underwrite portions of a loan. Another account allows people willing to donate funds over a period to do so by paying back a loan given to a project they support. The bank also runs target accounts where investors can specify the particular project or business they would like their money to be loaned to.

In 1995, Triodos entered into agreements with two religious groups. The Triodos Dana Partnership Account is a linkup with the Friends of the Western Buddhist Order. Money deposited by members of the Friends is in turn lent out to FWBO projects. Depositors opening a Triodos Quaker Social Housing Account know their money will be loaned to assist 'self build projects, housing co-operatives, homes meeting special needs, and initiatives to break the cycle of homelessness'. Both these funds operate as conventional deposit accounts, with normal bank protection and annual interest payments.

Triodos was also behind The Wind Fund PLC, an investment fund intended to loan money to small scale wind energy projects. These projects benefit from government requirements imposed on the electricity companies to buy from non fossil fuel sources and are beginning to make an effective contribution to lessening our reliance on fossil fuels and the nuclear industry.

All of this is a world away from the working practice of the high street banks. 'A lot of social investment has a negative orientation', says Triodos joint managing director Glen Saunders, 'but our approach is to look at what people are doing that is positive. Many of our projects could be criticised but the question is, what initiatives are they taking? What new step is being taken? Money is always dirty to some extent, so the question is, what can you do to make it better? We are not interested in projects which just obey the law: there must be social added value'.

The bank encourages people to become involved in projects they lend to, and Saunders cites examples of people who have agreed to target savings to a particular scheme, and then become actively involved in it.

Triodos' deposit accounts are probably more ethical than anything else offered by a bank in the UK. But while they are planning to introduce current accounts with chequebooks, they won't be issuing cheque guarantee cards. 'Our aim is not to provide every bell and whistle that the main banks offer', says Saunders. 'Money in current accounts is "fast money"; it has to be very liquid for it comes in at the beginning of the month and is out by the end. There is nothing social or environmental we can do with fast money. We want people's savings'. The current accounts with billpaying service and no guarantee cards are their way of responding to customers' needs, but without moving away from their central principle – to lend money to projects of social or environmental worth.

The Ecology Building Society

The EBS is a small building society which has established a growing reputation for lending 'for the purchase of ecologically-sound properties only'. They say advances are made to 'persons or on property which are most likely to lead to the saving of non-renewable resources, the promotion of self-sufficiency in individuals or communities, or the most ecologically efficient use of land. We are opposed to the wasteful use of land and resources encouraged by orthodox lending policies. We aim to contribute to the regeneration of rural areas and inner cities, and promote a more ecological way of life'.

The society says membership 'has a real meaning. Investors and borrowers tend to feel a sense of personal involvement with the Society and its ideals, recapturing perhaps something of the spirit which helped to found the building societies movement. The EBS is committed to a small-scale, concerned and mutually beneficial approach. An ecological way of life is not a pipe dream. It can, and has with our help, become a reality for an ever increasing number of people'.

This is all a far cry from the conventional building society which considers *only* whether the borrower can pay back the loan, and whether the property provides sufficient security if the borrower defaults. Among the properties the EBS has given mortgages on are small-scale workshops, back to back houses which 'by their nature are energy saving', homes for people running small businesses with an ecological bias such as paper recycling, and craft workshops, derelict but sound houses which would otherwise have been abandoned, houses which incorporate special energy saving or energy efficient features, organic smallholdings and farms, and properties which will help to promote the life of small communities.

The society's newsletter gives details of who they loan money to. Loans have supported a quadruple glazed and solar heated home in Suffolk, an office and home for Local Exchange Trading System members in Devon, a communal home for a housing co-operative in West Yorkshire, a traditional oak framed house in Dorset, and the restoration of a forge in a Tudor cottage in Warwickshire. Many loans fund combined homes and workplaces.

For savers, the society operates in a conventional way with interest paid regularly on accounts, and protection given by the Investors Protection Scheme which provides compensation to savers in most building societies in case of liquidation. They also sell bonds (see Chapter 6), and various other investment opportunities.

Why the trade union bank doesn't adopt an ethical policy

'The Unity Bank does not have personal customers and, as it is owned by the trade union movement, most of our customers are local trade union branches and affiliated organisations.

'Many of our trade union customers have members who work in industries, not all of which are environmentally friendly. GMB members work in the nuclear industry, RMT members transport nuclear waste, MSF members work in the tobacco industry and have members who experiment on animals in laboratories, TGWU members work in intensive livestock rearing and spray dangerous chemicals on the land. We have customers whose members drive juggernauts and aeroplanes, work on oil rigs and tip toxic waste into the sea. Unity Trust Bank cannot wrap itself in an 'ethical policy statement' or adopt an environmental code of practice that would impact on our customers' business.

'Whenever we have asked our customers what their views are with regard to ethical investment, the only constraint that they have put on us is that Unity should invest the bulk of its funds in the UK economy. The intention is for Unity's investments to create jobs and thereby help trades unions and their members who are our shareholders'.

Steve Billcliffe, Marketing Manager of the Unity Trust Bank
(and former Director of Friends of the Earth).

9

Investing in the social economy

●●●

'Merciful God, make me neither rich nor poor'.
The daily prayer of the Abbé Alphonse Lugan of St. Germain des Prés

RECENT YEARS HAVE seen a growth in what is becoming known as the 'social economy'. While most businesses and banks are run primarily for profit, businesses in the social economy are run primarily to supply the goods and services people need while making a contribution to human welfare or the environment, with any profits being a desirable extra.

This is not to say that such businesses are run less well than conventional companies, indeed in many cases the service the customer receives may be far better, and any adverse impact on the environment and the local community will be far less. In the conventional financial world, however, investment in the social economy is seen as high risk with only modest potential profits. From the point of view of the environment, local communities, customers, and workers, community businesses are often far more attractive organisations than the large anonymous multinationals increasingly dominating our economy.

The social economy spans housing associations; retail, distribution and manufacturing co-operatives; community development associations; fair trade organisations such as Traidcraft; and charities such as the Centre for Alternative Technology. None of the bodies operating within the social economy is listed on the Stock Exchange, though some are public companies, while most obtain another legal status such as that of a (private) limited company, workers' co-operative, or credit union.

The ethical advantages for the investor are high: and many savers putting money into one of these projects can be satisfied that their funds are being used for real social good. In addition, since these are mainly small organisations, there is not the fear that some obscure part of the company is involved in a line of work with which you fundamentally disagree. Placing money in the social economy also often allows the recipient to use your money as a springboard to obtain more. Many banks, for example, will lend to a social business only as much cash as it has obtained elsewhere.

The disadvantages are mainly on the financial side: the profits are likely to be modest, and because there is not an established market in buying and selling the shares and investments, you are likely to be reliant on the lists of prospective investors some of the companies maintain, rather than knowing you can sell them on easily and possibly at a profit as you can with shares on the stock market. (There is a need for a stock market dealing in the shares of social economy organisations – one where the share price does not fluctuate but where investors can sell and regain their cash if they need it).

Conventional financial advisers will also suggest the risk of large losses is higher in small financial organisations where a downturn in the market of one sector cannot be off-set by other more profitable parts of the company.

This view of the conventional financial world has meant that despite the rapid growth of ethical investment, social economy companies generally find it as difficult to gain investment funding as they ever did. This is both ironic and unfortunate, since many investors quite rightly want some or all of their money used for positive social good, and it is really only the social economy organisations which can meet high ethical criteria.

Recent years have seen the beginning of a merging between the commercial sector and the charities. The law governing the work of the latter is increasingly seen to be in need of reform: a charity can give money and goods away to the poor and needy, it can express some opinions on changes to the law needed to help the poor and needy, but it can't generally campaign to help them, and there are restrictions on charities helping to set up businesses so the poor and needy can help themselves.

Some charities are beginning to test these barriers, and have been setting up non-charitable arms to form businesses or provide funding. One even has government money to make loans to businesses providing social worth. To comply with the charities regulations, they can only lend to companies which aren't seeking to make a profit for individuals – and it is here that the social economy brings together charities and self help community businesses.

As with the stock market, the social economy can be divided into the businesses and co-operatives themselves and various types of investment funds. The funds invite investment from a wide range of individuals and institutions, and lend it to businesses, charities and co-operatives meeting their criteria.

The companies and co-ops

Here are some examples of businesses and projects which operate in the social economy.

Archway Resource Centre

The Archway Resource Centre is a group of buildings housing a number of environmental and social change organisations in North London. The centre provides accommodation at below market rents and a range of shared facilities such as photocopiers, fax machines, meeting rooms and computers. The aim is to provide organisations with a stable base, and to encourage them to build up mutual support networks.

In late 1995 the centre acquired three shop units adjoining their existing premises and have set up a Targeted Loan Facility with Triodos Bank (see Chapter 8). The facility will allow investors to open a deposit account with Triodos and direct that the money is loaned to the centre for the provision of the office services which many groups need. Investors will be able to choose the rate of interest they wish to receive which in turn will affect the rent and costs the occupying groups will have to pay.

The extra space is intended to benefit environmental, development and social change groups, and help particularly small and newly formed organisations. Groups already occupying space include the UK Green Party, the Islington Zairean Refugee Group, Small World (which provides media support for campaigning groups), and *Squall*, the magazine for 'sorted itinerants'.

Future plans for the centre include forming Britain's first ethical property investment company, the author being one of the directors.

The Barnet Green Co-op Ltd

This proposed shop in North London intends to sell what they term 'ecologically-sound products' and are appealing for supporters to buy £10 bonds which will entitle holders to a 10% discount on all shop purchases.

BARNET GREEN CO-OP LIMITED   SPECIMEN

ENVIRONMENTAL BOND   No: 2
Value £10

Issued to _____ Date _____

This bond has been issued to enable Barnet Green Co-op
to open a Green shop.
This bond can be redeemed at full face value
after a period of 1 year.
Bond holders are entitled to a 10% discount on goods.

For conditions see over

The bonds won't, however, pay interest and investors will be able to cash in the bonds after a year. The shop is an initiative by Barnet and Hendon Green Parties who intend using it as a way of keeping their prospective parliamentary candidate mixing with the public.

The co-op is aware their bonds may not be the safest of investments: their appeal for funds says to prospective investors: 'At this point you might be thinking: "Oh no, not another green right-on venture that will go bust in six weeks". But this is not a pie-in-the-sky venture. The co-op will be run on strictly business lines with a full-time manager who has retail experience'.

The shop has been set up as a company limited by guarantee, and hopes to promote the conversion of swords into ploughshares by taking on the lease of a former army careers information office.

Bioregional Charcoal Company Limited

The BRCC is a private limited company aiming to promote the supply of local woodland products, particularly charcoal, to national retail chains. The intention is to promote sustainable use of woodlands and create local employment.

The company was set up by the Bioregional Development Group, an environmental charity, to bring together local charcoal burners into a national network to supply to the chain B&Q. Hitherto B&Q had sourced most of its charcoal from abroad, much of it from tropical forests, and the local charcoal scheme is intended to replace this.

In Spring 1996 the BRCC raised £25,000 through the sale of £1 non-voting shares, and aims to raise a further £50,000 in 1997. The set-up of the company means the Bioregional Development Group will keep the voting shares while the dividends are paid to investors owning the non-voting shares.

The Centre for Alternative Technology PLC (CAT)

CAT describes itself as 'Europe's leading practical proponent of ecological lifestyles', which 'plays an important part in informing and inspiring people of all ages about the possibility for sustainable life on earth. The Centre has a mission of the utmost importance – to invite the ever increasing numbers of those concerned about their environment to experience new ways of living in harmony with the planet'. It does this by educating, informing and inspiring citizens and governments to build towards a low energy, fossil-free society where all resources are sustainably managed.

The flotation of shares in 1990 was designed to raise £1m to pay for a water powered cliff railway, an audio-visual introductory theatre, shop, café, lecture room, exhibition and landscaping. The flotation was wholly successful in that all the shares sold, and the offer therefore technically closed. Although the Centre has made a profit in the years since the flotation, shareholders have voted to return the gains to CAT and not take a dividend.

There are still limited opportunities for investors wishing to support CAT's work as they maintain a running list of prospective buyers and sellers of shares so that people who bought in at the date of flotation can sell their shares on if they need to recover their money. However, unlike companies listed on the stock market, the shares do not rise or fall in price: they sell at the £1 each originally paid for them.

'The Co-op'

It is a matter of opinion whether the Co-operative shops are really part of the social economy. The shops grew out of the work of the Rochdale Pioneers in the last century and they were set up on a wave of self-help philosophies to allow working people to buy good quality food at reasonable prices, with profits divided among the members. People become members by buying shares, and unlike conventional companies, each member had one vote irrespective of the size of the shareholding. The Co-op shops are consumer co-operatives; that is, their customer-members are the owners, unlike worker co-operatives where it is the employees who take the decisions.

There are now many hundreds of Co-op shops grouped in about 50 independent societies, the two largest chains being Co-operative Retail Services and (despite its name) the Co-operative Wholesale Society. They still adhere to their principles of democracy among members and workers, but the range of goods sold on the shelves is broadly the same as that found in other supermarkets. The Co-ops, while they claim to have adopted ethical and environmental statements, still run out-of-town superstores deliberately placed near motorways, and sell the usual mix of foods with additives and decorative packaging. CRS does, however, claim to have been the first retailer to have stopped stocking goods from South Africa during the boycott.

'A tidy investment' is one of the rewards offered to members who invest in Co-operative Retail Services, one of the largest Co-op chains. CRS has over a million members and owns a range of 'neighbourhood supermarkets', giant superstores, home furnishing centres, department stores and one of the largest funeral businesses in the UK.

Investments operate like bank deposit accounts; interest is paid, but with the money being used by the Co-op society as working capital. The society says: 'CRS applies the co-operative principle of democratic control so members can have a say in the way the Society is run through annual regional members' meetings and locally elected committees which elect the board of directors'. Deposits in CRS attracted annual interest of 6.4% in 1996 with the traditional co-op 'divi' – available now as a 5% discount on non-food purchases – credited to the savings account. The Oxford, Swindon and Gloucester Co-op pays (June 1996) 6.25% gross interest on deposits as low as £200, but the ethical investor has to be happy that this Co-op runs a number of garages selling imported cars and could put the investment into a new dealership rather than corner shops or an organic farm to supply its fruit and veg. Some societies also offer bonds for longer term savers.

The Co-ops support a number of community activities such as the Woodcraft Folk (a co-educational green version of the scouts and guides), a Young People's Film and Video Festival, and links with groups such as Oxfam.

In some ways the Co-ops are a hangover from the days when they were seen as a bastion against the exploitative free market. There's no doubt that members have opportunities to influence society policy which customers of other supermarket chains don't have, but few would claim the Co-op shops are at the leading edge of ethical shopping or investment.

Concern about whether the Co-op has lost its way has spawned the National Federation of Progressive Co-operators which aims to 'rebuild the concept of partnership to show co-operation is an economic, social and political force which works'. The Federation acts as a pressure group within the movement and aims to restore the principles which were behind the formation of the first Co-op shops.

Housing co-operatives

These are non-profit making institutions set up to provide housing for their members. They are normally registered with the Registrar of Friendly Societies and seek funds to buy run-down properties or build from scratch. They then normally rent the homes to members at below market rents.

Some co-ops issue loan stock to members and sympathisers. These are loans from individuals which are used to buy property or pay for rehabilitation. While such loans are likely to meet most ethical criteria, they have the disadvantage of not being easily recovered by the investor – the money having been sunk into bricks and mortar.

Consequently, they are not 'secure investments' and the law governing investments actually prohibits them being described as such. They may pay interest if the co-op has agreed to do so, and is generating sufficient rent to – but not all co-ops are able or willing to.

However co-ops are generally open organisations and an investor planning to buy loan stock would usually have the opportunity to meet the people administering the organisation and assess their effectiveness directly – an opportunity rarely available in the conventional financial world.

Such co-ops include Ecogroco based in Cornwall, Phoenix (MK) in Milton Keynes, and Cornerstone in Leeds.

Ecogroco offer loanstock to people who can invest for five years, and they say they will pay a maximum interest rate of 4% with money deposited with the Ecology Building Society (see Chapter 8) until it is needed to purchase property. Minimum investment is £50. Ecogroco says: 'Many of our environmental and social problems are caused by the way we live and where we live. Ecogroco wants to illustrate how many of these problems can be alleviated with simple changes to our lifestyle and housing. By providing decent, affordable and secure rented accommodation, Ecogroco hopes to create a safe environment in which adults and children can live, work, grow, play and learn together, developing a creative sustainable community based on the principles of mutual aid. Not a commune, but a village structure of separate inter-dependent dwellings, with a larger central building providing the option of a shared space'.

Other housing co-ops have less extensive aims, merely existing to provide housing and giving the occupants a chance to make decisions over their living space.

The Ecological Trading Company PLC

The ETC was set up to import sustainably grown, mainly tropical timber into the UK and thereby benefit local people and not destroy the natural environment. The company describes itself as an 'alternative trading organisation specialising in the importation and processing of timber from sustainable sources.

'ETC works with small and medium scale community based projects. Community members are encouraged to undertake the forestry operations themselves and therefore receive a far greater proportion of the benefits than would be the case if they relinquished control of their lands to others.

'For people to make use of their natural environment in a way which can be sustained over a long period, they must have the opportunity to do so. In other words, it must be possible for them to sustain themselves, their families, and their society in a way which does not destroy their natural environment. If we look at the issue of sustainability from this perspective, it appears that sustainability is not all about saving trees or butterflies; it is about people trying to make a living and it is about the social, economic and political conditions under which they have to do this'.

ETC is an unquoted company – that is, its shares are not traded on the Stock Exchange – and there are no compensation arrangements for investors if the necessary business is not forthcoming.

Out Of This World

A prospectus inviting investment in a chain of shops doesn't usually include the provision of 'fun' as a principal ingredient. Yet Out of This World aims to make its chain of ethical and environmentally sound shops 'interesting, stimulating, attractive and fun – but serious fun'. The company is the brain-child of Richard Adams, the founder of the fair trading company Traidcraft, and the ethical magazine *New Consumer*.

Out of This World launched a fund to raise £1m to finance the development of the chain of shops selling products with an ethical, social or environmental dimension – 'organic, cruelty free, fair trade, healthy eating, additive free, low impact and energy efficient'.

The aim is to open about 12 shops in three years, each selling about 3000 products including food, household consumables such as cleaning materials and light bulbs, household durables such as electrical appliances and furniture, DIY goods such as paint and wallpaper, clothing and footwear, crafts and gifts, jewellery, cosmetics and toiletries, stationery, health products, and leisure goods such as books and computers.

They stress that unlike charity shops, the staff will not be volunteers: 'the shops will be run professionally, in all the best senses of that word. They will be staffed by people who believe in being the best and in the importance of detail in doing a job well'.

Part of the company's aim is to forge a link between shoppers and the shops, and thus Out of This World is set up so customers need to become members before they can purchase goods.

The investment opportunities involve becoming a member by buying shares in the company. Each member has one vote, irrespective of the number of shares owned. Those investing more than £250 can select a rate of interest between zero and 10%. The Industrial and Provident Societies Act which regulates Out of This World specifies that the price of the shares cannot fluctuate. They can be transferred, but can only be sold back to OOTW when the business make a profit, which is estimated to be five years after the launch in 1995. Interest will be credited to accounts from the date the shares are bought, but will only be paid when the business is profitable.

Paperback Ltd.

Paperback distributes and promotes the use of recycled paper and operates as a workers' co-op. In 1988 they invited investors to lend them money by buying loanstock in units of £100. The loanstock is still available and pays a minimum interest rate of 5% and a maximum of about 12%, the level being linked to profitability. The stock must be held for a minimum period of five years after which Paperback will pay back the investor.

Owning the loanstock gives no voting power to the holders as Paperback is registered as an Industrial and Provident Society with all control resting with the employees. However owners of loanstock nominate a representative who periodically visits the company to pass on advice and views.

Red Pepper

This is a monthly political magazine aiming to provide a 'pluralist voice for the radical green left'. It provides the usual mix of news and features on grassroots campaigns and what the editor, Hilary Wainwright, terms 'feasible Utopias'.

Investing in *Red Pepper* through the medium of shares is better seen as supporting a cause than gaining profit on your money. As with all new business ventures, the magazine does not expect to break even until it has traded for several years, and they give no undertaking to buy shares back. They expect dividends to be minimal, although the company has been set up under the auspices of the Enterprise Investment Scheme which gives some tax advantages to investors. The magazine will also accept loans which are individually negotiated.

Swanage Family Housing Association

Most housing associations obtain their funding from the government (via the Housing Corporation), local authorities or the banks. However the Swanage Family Housing Association in Dorset has set up an innovative scheme to harness the savings of local people. The Association began by leasing houses and renting them to homeless families. They then unsuccessfully sought commercial loans and Housing Corporation funds to purchase their own houses. Offers of loans from local residents then led them to invite loans for the purchase of houses, with projections that income from rents set at housing benefit levels would bring in interest of about 6% – similar to a building society. To provide flexibility, loans are limited to £5000 or 10% of each property's value. Higher value loans are accepted but they are spread across several properties.

The aim of the Association is to provide 'affordable' housing for local Swanage families with low incomes. It is a charity and registered as an Industrial and Provident Society.

At the time of writing the Association's investment fund was at an early stage, but its plans are likely to be keenly watched by other housing associations eager to raise funds beyond those available from conventional sources.

Traidcraft PLC

Traidcraft is a 'fair trade' organisation which exists 'to expand and establish trading systems which are more just and which express the principles of love and justice'. It imports and distributes handicrafts, fashion goods, stationery, drinks and food from the Third World. Most of the producer groups it buys from are community based enterprises and associations of smallholder farmers. Traidcraft has undoubtedly assisted many otherwise destitute people to find work.

Its associated charitable company, Traidcraft Exchange, helps producers with product and business development, marketing information and training.

The company prides itself on its Christian base and pays prices for its goods which cover not only production costs but also the producers' basic needs. It tries to foster a long term relationship with the producers by holding to agreed prices and making advance payments. In the UK much of the selling is carried out by their 2000 voluntary representatives.

Traidcraft was one of the first social economy companies to gain PLC status. Its shares were all sold when the company went public, but it maintains a list of prospective sellers of shares which is provided to prospective buyers. The shares can increase in value but most change hands at the original face value. Small dividends have been paid by the company but not in recent years. The intention is to pay dividends when the company's profit allows it, although a number of shareholders have stated they do not wish to receive dividends.

The funds

Aston Reinvestment Trust

ART SHARE (Self Help Association for Reinvesting in Enterprise) describe themselves as being a 'rebuilding society', similar to a building society but lending money for businesses and housing needs. They intend to launch in 1996 with both borrowers and lenders as members and with the aim of investing in projects within central Birmingham. ART SHARE will lend to five different sectors: affordable housing, energy efficiency, charities, small businesses, and 'micro-businesses' – broadly the self-employed. They will only lend to projects with 'social or environmental value' and a long term plan is to provide loans with varying payback arrangements to take account of the good times and bad times some businesses face.

Their plans for lending to micro-businesses are probably the most imaginative. The people who find it the most difficult to borrow money for businesses are those on very low incomes. Since many in this group survive on social security and do not own their own homes, they generally find it impossible to borrow money from conventional sources as they cannot produce security. ART SHARE intend to form groups of about half a dozen prospective entrepreneurs who would save regular sums with the ART Self Employment Loan Fund and then decide between them which of their businesses would receive the first loan. This would be a very small sum – perhaps as little as £250 and the group would oversee the repayments of each individual. As the individuals establish a track record they could apply for higher loans, and other members of the group could too. This plan follows in the steps established by the highly successful Grameen

Bank in Bangladesh which has shown that such borrowing communities can make it highly safe to lend to the very poor.

ART SHARE are also planning to lend to a 'foyer' development which would provide housing for 80 young homeless people with training workshops built in, and to develop a Birmingham Energy Savers Fund. Investors are able to buy shares in ARTSHARE and the intention is to pay annual dividends in a similar way to credit unions (see below).

Charities Aid Foundation (CAF)

CAF's Social Investment Fund allows individuals to invest lump sums with CAF which are loaned to registered charities.

The aim is not to provide investment opportunities producing profit for individuals, but to allow them to lend money to charities and recover it if necessary. The charities in turn gain access to money at an affordable rate.

To distinguish the funds from conventional investments, CAF call the deposits 'Returnable Donations' and donors pledge the money for a set period of time. The Fund was only opened in late 1995 and government regulations bar the payment of interest to donors, but the trustees say that once it is established they will consider applying for legal approval to pay interest.

Credit unions

There are over 500 credit unions operative in the UK, and 15 of them have assets of over £1m. They operate only within a community of people with a common bond – covering a town or employees of a company. Members agree to save a particular sum each week, and after they have built up a certain level of savings, they become eligible to borrow up to specified multiples of this amount. Dividends are paid to savers and interest charged to borrowers – but at generally lower rates than commercial lending institutions. The union is non-profit making and owned and controlled by the members, and many of them use volunteers to undertake the administration.

Credit unions have been performing useful work providing credit to people particularly in poor areas who find it difficult to obtain small bank loans, and who may otherwise be forced to borrow at much higher interest rates.

For the investor, the credit unions are a useful way of building up a nest-egg. However, once your money is in the credit union's account, some of it is deposited in a commercial lending institution: credit unions do not claim that they invest their money in ethical ways, merely that they lend it out to members who need to borrow. The Association of British Credit Unions suggests to member unions that they use the Co-operative Bank to deposit money not loaned to individuals, and they stress that if members believe funds are being placed in non-ethical accounts, they can press the credit union to adopt an ethical investment policy. The unions cannot, however, deposit money other than in banks, building societies, or government bonds, because of legal restrictions. The annual conference of the Association of British Credit Unions has urged member societies to invest their funds ethically.

Industrial Common Ownership Finance (ICOF)

ICOF Community Capital is a fund which lends to 'businesses that are concerned as much with people as with profit, including those that pursue environmental improvement, provide facilities in rural areas, and regenerate inner cities. The pursuit of equal opportunities, social justice and sound business practice, will be ICOF's hallmarks'.

ICOF itself has been in existence for over twenty-one years and describes itself as 'one of the early pioneers of ethical investment'. This is a justified claim since the well known ethical funds – the unit trusts – only began operating a decade ago. It specialises in loaning money to common ownership and worker co-operatives and began with £250,000 from the government in 1976 which established it as the 'national body for co-operative finance'. Most of its funds came from local authorities wanting to encourage co-ops, but its Community Capital Fund aims to harness money from individual savers. While ICOF retains its commitment to co-ops, it now lends to other organisations promoting social justice.

ICOF is a business, and not a charity, though it is not listed on the Stock Exchange. It says it 'will be investing in social economy businesses which are viable and operate in a commercially effective and efficient manner. We recognise that their level of profitability may be constrained by the achievement of social or environmental profit and we expect our investors to share this recognition. This is an ethical investment with a priority for people rather than profit. We believe there is a growing body of people who share this view and who wish to commit some of their resources to community and social enterprises with the expectation of lower financial return'.

The Fund's prospectus describes loans given to a city farm; a community cinema; a transport company for the elderly, disabled and housebound; and a nursery. Most of the loans have been made to businesses operating in deprived areas.

Shares in the Community Capital Fund are priced at £1 each, with minimum subscriptions of £250. There is no opportunity for selling the shares on at a profit, with the Fund undertaking to buy back shares after being given six months notice. Ownership of shares gives members the right to participate in ICOF's decision making structure on the basis of one person, one vote, regardless of the size of the shareholding. The fund has a 'target' to offer interest 'approximately in line with inflation'.

Local Investment Fund (LIF)

The LIF is a partnership between companies with social concerns and the Department of the Environment, brought together by Business in the Community. In late 1994 they set up the the Local Investment Fund with money from the DoE and a number of large public companies. The aim of the fund is to give loans to 'community based enterprises which are economically viable but cannot obtain conventional financing on reasonable terms because of a lack of track record or asset base. The fund will encourage voluntary bodies which have a viable project to move from depending on grants to loan-based financing'. They also aim to 'test new financing mechanisms to support community regeneration and to forge productive and continuing alliances between community organisations and the local and national private sector'.

As the fund is a registered charity it can only lend to organisations promoting social worth and not private profit and whose aims comply with statutory charitable objectives. In 1996, when they hope the fund will have proved its merit, they intend to boost the sums available by appealing to individual investors to lend money in return for fixed interest rates.

Loans granted by 1996 included one for an organisation to buy a derelict building to house a local Family Service Unit, one for the provision of a building to provide respite care, and a third assisting the formation of a construction company employing and training unemployed people in a deprived area.

The fund's board is due to consider proposals to maintain the liquid portion of their funds (that component not already on loan) in an ethical portfolio.

Radical Routes

Radical Routes is a co-operative set up to provide financial and other services to housing and worker co-ops. Among these services is a scheme whereby individuals invest with Radical Routes, and the money is lent out to the member co-operatives.

Radical Routes say their money goes to 'rural co-ops involved in organic agriculture as well as urban co-op businesses, to housing co-ops providing accommodation as well as worker co-ops providing socially useful work'.

Investors can choose the interest rate they require, from zero to approaching the current commercial rate.

While commercial banks and lending institutions give little or no details of where their money is lent, Radical Routes' newsletter describes the co-ops where it is investing money. Most of the loans are under £10,000, and include funds passed to a recycling network, a builders co-op aiming to provide homes for homeless people, an organic vegetable delivery service, and farms run on permaculture principles.

In early 1996 Radical Routes invited investment in a new issue of unsecured loanstock. They were seeking to raise £250,000 in £10 units paying interest of between zero and 4% and repayable in 2001.

Every debt a good debt

Radical Routes said in 1996 that they had never had a bad debt from a loan to a member co-operative. This is a loans record which most banks would envy.

They explain that conventional banks will only lend if the key people involved have their own money to put up as security. Most co-ops are set up by people who have little money of their own and 'this is how poor people all over the world are denied access to credit'. They continue: 'More enlightened organisations who do not impose this restriction may show a lower rate of bad debts than conventional banks – yet the traditional conservatism remains'.

Radical Routes try and loan money in conjunction with other sympathetic bodies, and thus they claim their loans have a knock-on benefit beyond the comparatively small sums they deal in.

The Scottish Community Enterprise Investment Fund PLC

This fund aims to 'raise funds for investment in Scottish Community Enterprises by acting as the main channel for people and organisations wishing to give financial assistance to people tackling local economic and employment problems. The social benefits are to improve community morale, to give back a sense of pride and achievement to some of Scotland's most disadvantaged communities, to improve local services and to use profits for schemes of local community benefit'.

They warn, however, that 'the financial return which investors can expect from the fund is small. Community Enterprise Shares are not intended to be a conventional investment. There is no prospect of the capital value of the shares increasing and there are significant risk factors involved'.

Annual dividends are payable, and the articles of association specify that they shall only be up to 5% – and the directors (not the shareholders) decide how much. Shareholders can require the company to buy them back after a certain number of years. In late 1995 all the shares had been issued, but the fund planned to issue more shares in Autumn 1996.

While the social and ethical standards of individual businesses are paramount to the fund, investors with particular concerns such as objections to alcohol sales would need to check which types of businesses were being given loans.

Shared Interest

Shared Interest describes itself as a 'social investment society' whose aim is to provide investment for the benefit of poor people in the Third World.

They aim to invest in sustainable enterprises which can service and repay capital but whose business and profits 'serve the interest of the poor rather than the rich, usually through charitable, co-operative or community ownership'. Two thirds of the funds are invested abroad, with the remainder guaranteeing loans to development trusts in the UK which undertake similar work.

Shared Interest says: 'People are poor because they or their families cannot earn a decent living. Sometimes this is for natural or political reasons, like sickness, drought or civil war. Often, especially in the Third World, they are denied access to markets, business credit and employment. There are many enterprises in the Third World which are run by or for people who are disadvantaged in material terms. These enterprises face serious obstacles in the form of entrenched vested interests and lack of basic services. Shared Interest helps people who lack basic necessities to earn a better living with business loans that they cannot obtain locally on fair terms. People in the Third World want a relationship built on trust and confidence, a source of dignity and independence: a relationship where power is shared'.

Money is provided through a range of networks including fair trade organisations such as Traidcraft and Oxfam Trading. Among the products available on UK shop shelves, Shared Interest money has assisted Cafédirect coffee from a co-operative of small farmers in Latin America; Mascao chocolate from a co-operative of 1000 cocoa producers in the Bolivian rainforest; and Tropical Forest Organic Honey from a beekeeper co-operative in Tanzania. These co-ops provide loans during the growing season, transport and storage at harvest, processing and packaging, and access to national and international markets. Shared Interest says that crops such as honey helps to deter the clearance of tropical forests for the growing of cash crops such as tobacco.

For investors, the accounts operate like those of a building society with interest paid regularly and withdrawal available on demand – though the Fund warns it is not part of any investor compensation schemes. The interest rate is generally lower than that paid by conventional building societies – which allows them to charge lower rates to the organisations they lend to.

In addition to its normal share account, the fund offers loan stock for investments of over £2000, with an optional guarantee from the Co-operative Bank.

Shared Interest put ethics high on their agenda and their literature addresses questions such as whether their loans add to Third World debt, and where they hold their money before it is loaned out: 'cash not specifically applied is held primarily with the Co-operative Bank and with building societies. Where possible, we avoid dealing with banks which have contributed to the Third World debt burden'.

Shared Interest also put ethics before the offer of a $2m loan and $450,000 grant from the international currency trader, George Soros. His Soros Foundation offered these sums to Shared Interest's then international partners for investing in projects set up by the poor in Eastern Europe. There were no strings attached to the loan, but the money had come from Soros' speculation against the pound in the international currency exchange markets. Shared Interest recommended that the loan be refused on the grounds that while it would be beneficial in the short term to poor people in Eastern Europe, speculation 'is one of the causes of world poverty' and their aim is to 'demonstrate that business can be done ethically'.

The discussions aroused much concern within Shared Interest and its partners, but the bottom line was that they put ethical principles above a very large sum of money. As such they are a world apart from conventional banking and finance houses.

Shared Visions

This is a company intending to launch in Spring 1996 which will provide financial and business expertise and loans to sustainable businesses. It is the brainchild of activists in the Permaculture movement and their aim is to assist businesses and organisations which 'care for the earth, care for people, and give fair shares'. Investors will be able to buy shares and the founders have set up an imaginative way to weight the control. Investors are entitled to buy one voting share per year of membership up to a maximum of seven: thus control of the company rests mainly with the founders for the first years, and gradually spreads further after that.

Investments will be through non-voting shares costing £250 each and the first loan is likely to be provided to a project aiming to teach both ordinary people and professionals about sustainable building techniques.

An imaginative aspect of the company will be their way of assisting loan applicants to obtain business and financial advice. They intend to use specialists to give this advice who would be paid with shares in the company. They hope this form of 'sweat equity' – using people's labour to replace capital – will allow new businesses to receive professional expertise they would not otherwise be able to afford. It will also assist Shared Vision to more accurately assess the economic viability of prospective borrowers.

Shared Vision is being set up as a conventional company limited by shareholder, but with the special arrangement regarding voting shares.

Tools for Self Reliance Cymru (TFSR)

TFSR is a charity whose supporters collect and refurbish tools for distribution to community groups in the Third World.

The Crickhowell group are buying a semi-derelict barn in a new tele-village/craft centre in mid Wales. They intend converting it to a permanent workshop for restoring tools. The group receive requests from community organisations in rural areas in six African countries and refurbish several hundred tools a year. Tools they are given which are not required abroad (African farmers use their own design of hoes rather than spades and forks) are sold to raise funds in the UK. They thus provide a useful recycling initiative too.

The group need loans to fund the £28,000 needed to buy, rehabilitate and equip the new workshops. They particularly welcome interest-free loans.

Totnes Investment in Local Trade (TILT)

TILT is a small local investment fund operating in and around the Devon town of Totnes. It was set up to 'put money into locally controlled ventures which benefit the community and the environment'.

They say: 'Investors in TILT believe there is more to be had out of investment than quick financial profit. If the projects being supported carry through schemes which improve the investor's surroundings, the investor is deriving more than purely financial interest from the loan...What is the use to an investor, for instance, of making sufficient profit through conventional investment to buy a sailing dinghy if the coastline where it sails happens to be polluted by the companies which the investment supported? Likewise what is the use to the investor of making profits if the economic trends to which his or her investment contributes, are responsible for deprivation that leads to hostility and vandalism?'

The fund provides loans which are fully secured and they have had no defaulters among the nine loans provided. Money has been lent to a joinery workshop using local hardwoods, and a photographer and artist who contributes to a macrobiotic magazine.

TILT (like Shared Visions – see above) uses an ingenious method of rewarding long term commitment. They encourage people to become members for the price of a £10 voting share. These members shape the policy of the fund, and they can buy more voting shares at the rate of one per year up to a maximum of five. Most of the funds come, however, from the purchase of non-voting ordinary shares, which, like the loans, can only be allocated to members.

The Wind Company Ltd

This is a co-operative set up by the Swedish company Vindkompaniet AB which has been responsible for installing locally owned wind energy farms.

Their first UK project is in Cumbria and will consist of five turbines with shares being sold mainly to people in Furness, South Lakeland, Cumbria and Lancashire. The company, which is a registered co-operative, has been set up under the government's Enterprise Investment Scheme which gives some tax benefits to investors, and the electricity generated will be bought under the terms of a government contract called the Non-Fossil Fuel Obligation.

The Wind Fund PLC

This is one of the many initiatives from Triodos Bank (see Chapter 8) and aims to 'provide equity funding for small-scale renewable energy projects in the UK'. They say: 'Wind energy is our first priority as wind is an abundant resource and the technologies for wind energy generation have reached a mature stage in their development. We believe that wind energy is environmentally benign and leaves no damaging legacy. With costs coming down it is prospectively a competitive contributor to Britain's energy needs. The Wind Fund offers individuals a direct way of taking practical action for the environment'.

The Fund has adopted a code of practice stating that it will support renewable energy projects which 'are commercially viable, minimise financial risk through the use of mature technologies and do not create any measurable atmospheric pollutants during operation; which minimise environmental impact through sensitive siting; which minimise operational impact on local communities; and which can demonstrate a meaningful public consultation process'.

These standards aim to address the concerns of many communities which gain little directly from conventional wind farm development – the income going to the wind energy company, and the community not even benefiting from low cost electricity.

Minimum investment is £300 and the Fund warns that dividends are unlikely to be payable until 1997. The company is not listed on the Stock Exchange and the directors will keep a running list of prospective buyers and sellers of shares – but like most such companies, the shares may rise or fall in value. Investors will be able to nominate particular renewable energy projects they would like their money to support.

Going for the humdinger?

These are all companies and organisations with a legal status which allows them to seek investment funding from the public. However, there is nothing to stop investors lending money to any business whose work they sympathise with, and which they are confident will use the money wisely.

Such investments are among the riskiest there are, and among providers of 'venture capital' the view is that of every six investments made, three will rapidly go bust, there will be one plodder, one will do quite well, and one will be a humdinger. But most investors will find it very difficult to survey a business – or especially a prospective business – to find one of the last two.

The rule, therefore, is not to invest more than you are prepared to lose.

The benefits, however, in investing in businesses known to you are that they are more likely to be small (and small businesses have the potential to create more and better jobs than large ones) and you will be able to meet the moving forces behind the business to assess whether they are really people you want to hand your money over to.

Like all investments, make sure you confirm in writing the terms of the loan and when and how it is expected to be repaid.

Triodos Match

This is another initiative by Triodos Bank and is intended to bring together projects and businesses seeking equity funding – principally by the issue of shares. Triodos Match is launching in Autumn 1996 and will comprise a newsletter published at least twice a year and a supporting database. Both will include details of projects of social and environmental worth and the sums of money they need. Triodos stress that inclusion of a project doesn't mean the bank is recommending it to investors, and that people considering buying shares need to be aware that if a business fails they could lose their money.

Private Equity Funding Association (PEFA)

PEFA exists to bring together entrepreneurs seeking capital with individual investors keen to put their money to profitable use. Entrepreneurs have to submit their business plans to the association for vetting, and if approved, details of the proposed business are circulated in the PEFA journal to prospective investors. The funding normally provided is in the form of equity capital – that is, the investor buys part of the business and shares in the profits, rather than loaning money against security. The shares issued are not listed on the Stock Exchange.

PEFA does not adopt ethical standards during the process but among the businesses needing funding are those seeking to manufacture or sell items with an environmental or social benefit. Investors would need to assess whether a particular business conformed to the desired ethical standards.

10

The financial advisers – independent and otherwise

●●●

'Mrs Banks (widowed, aged 36) has £350,000 in a high interest bank account. She had always relied on her husband to provide an income until his death; she has never worked and does not intend to start now'.
Introduction to specimen exam question for financial advisers,
The Chartered Insurance Institute, 1994.

T HE WORLD OF financial advice is yet another part of the financial services industry that is wrapped up in much mystique. However, unlike those working in most sectors, the financial advisers are usually the only people most investors will talk with face to face about where to place their money.

Broadly, financial advisers want to know the risk you are prepared to accept; when you want your money back; whether you want the interest or dividends to produce a regular income or to be added to the capital sum and received later; tax issues; and insurance.

Advisers say that factors such as the number and ages of any dependents, the age you intend to retire, your desire to buy expensive possessions such as a house or car, and whether you are employed or self-employed, make every individual's financial needs different. Thus they claim to produce advice tailored to your individual circumstances.

Advisers are required by law to choose whether to be tied to a particular financial company (working as their agent) or 'independent' and offering financial products from a range of companies. Most advisers opt for independent status and earn most of their income from commissions on the products they sell rather than from the giving of advice itself.

However, although the word independent appears prominently on their office doors and letterheads, an investor expecting to be receive advice across the whole range of opportunities will be disappointed. In general, advisers only give advice on unit trusts, pensions, life assurance, and PEPs: they don't involve themselves in assisting investors to buy shares in companies, whether quoted on the Stock Exchange or not, or in funds which invest in non-quoted companies such as those involved in the social economy (see Chapter 9).

This discrepancy exists because of differences in commission arrangements whereby unit trusts, pensions and similar schemes pay the adviser commission on sales, while banks and building societies do not. Because of these differences the advisers generally do not seek the necessary legal qualification to allow them to advise on the non-stock market investments.

In recent years a number of advisers have begun to specialise in offering advice on ethical investments. But while these ethical financial advisers may sometimes 'explain' about such organisations as the Ecology Building Society and Triodos Bank, these are unlikely to be put at the top of investment opportunities in the way pensions and unit trusts will. A number of advisers interviewed for this book hadn't even *heard of* funds such as Radical Routes and Business in the Community's Local Investment Fund. This glass wall between the financial advisers and the social economy is probably the biggest obstacle slowing the development of businesses of social and environmental worth.

The rates of commission paid by the large institutions also vary, and clients can find it difficult to know whether a particular investment is being recommended because it pays a higher commission than another similar plan.

Those in the financial services industry who are concerned about how commission payments can affect the advice given suggest that a solution is for clients to pay a set fee to the advisers. By working for a fee, the adviser is not open to the accusation that certain investments have been recommended because they pay high commissions. When an investor opts to pay a fee, any commission the adviser would have earned is generally credited to the investor's account instead. If the investor bypasses the financial adviser altogether the financial institution keeps the commission and it is not credited to the investor. However there is (understandable) reluctance from clients to pay a fee in this way, although some advisers do offer this facility.

Most of the ethical advisers will also advise on non-ethical funds. They do so because they argue that there is still not the full range of financial arrangements available with ethical options, and that for some customers, a non-ethical fund might be the most appropriate. Several advisers point to the absence of any ethical 'with profits' pension plans (plans which invest in company shares, government bonds, cash and property and which are of a low risk) as the main gap in the ethical market. However, the one adviser who makes a point of *only* advising on ethical and green investments – Lee Coates – argues that there are ethical financial plans carrying similar risk and offering similar returns as the with profits pensions – but these alternatives don't pay commission to the advisers.

The ethical advisers will only advise on financial matters, and they won't give advice on the ethical issues themselves. The usual approach is to ask clients about any ethical concerns and then seek appropriate investments. Many ethical advisers look somewhat askance at fellow ethical advisers who are far more pro-active in these matters. Several advisers stress they are 'listeners, not preachers' on ethical issues – 'unlike some in the industry'.

These factors mean the advisers broadly have to 'trust' the quality of the institutional fund managers, and work only within the current consensus of views of how the economy will perform. Most advisers – ethical as well as mainstream – are likely to be reluctant to advise from an investment point of view on issues such as the effects of global warming on the carbon fuel industry (see Chapter 5). Yet issues such as these are likely to have a profound effect on funds investing in this sector.

How suitable is suitable?

Few mainstream financial advisers bother to ask clients whether they have any ethical concerns. A survey at a conference of advisers confirmed that very few inquire about these concerns and when they are discussed, it is because the client requests information.

One adviser told the survey team: 'What one person considers ethical, another person considers unethical, so some people may be against alcohol, and tobacco, with others it's gambling, and others it's arms, there are just so many issues – it's very difficult actually to have any uniformity'.

Such comments are strange bearing in mind that advisers plead that their financial services are needed *precisely because* all investors' needs are different. It also shows that advisers are ignoring the finding in a Friends Provident survey that 83% of investors think advisers should ask them about their ethical concerns before recommending investments. It also ignores the Financial Services Act which requires advisers to recommend investments which are 'suitable' for the investor.

Similarly, advisers are unlikely to comment on the future viability of investments in the insurance industry – an area believed to be teetering on the edge of a financial abyss because of huge claims from asbestos victims and owners of contaminated land in the US. Such claims are believed to add up to more than the total assets of the insurance industry, meaning investors would want to think carefully before investing in these areas. But the make-up of the financial advice industry is such that even the green financial advisers will be unable to really assist investors on these issues.

Furthermore, although the advisers with 'independent' status are not tied to one particular company, in practice they only deal with a small number of the available institutions. This is because the complexities of many of the financial contracts are such that advisers find it difficult to keep up with the huge number of funds available, and because they will establish a rapport with particular funds and fund managers and will direct most business to them.

The Personal Investment Authority

Individuals and companies providing financial advice or services are required by law to be regulated. The government body responsible is the Securities and Investments Board and they have appointed the PIA to regulate the work of those offering financial services to the general public. The PIA is actually a private company (PIA Ltd) and its aim is 'to protect investors by the regulation and supervision of the retail investment sector, enabling investors to make properly informed decisions in an open, competitive, and innovative marketplace'.

It *only* regulates financial activities defined by the 1986 Financial Services Act which comprise: life insurance and endowment policies, personal pensions, unit trusts, Personal Equity Plans, guaranteed income bonds, investment trust savings schemes, offshore funds (funds invested abroad), advice on and arranging deals in shares quoted on the Stock Exchange, managing investment portfolios, broker funds, advice on Enterprise Investment Schemes, and advice on trading options.

The PIA has no responsibility for shares in companies not quoted on the Stock Exchange, co-operatives, mortgages (unless connected with an investment), bank and building society deposits, and general insurance such as for the household or vehicles.

Although the PIA regulates a wide range of financial contracts, members register under particular categories which allow them to conduct only particular types of business.

Most financial advisers register to advise only on collective investment schemes such as unit trusts, pensions, life assurance, and personal equity plans. Most do not seek registration which would allow them to buy quoted company shares directly for clients, or even advise on them.

According to the regulations, advisers are required to take account of the stated needs and circumstances of the individual client and advise on investments which are 'suitable'. A spokesman for the PIA confirms that ethical criteria when raised by the investor must be considered by the adviser. Thus if an investor states they do not wish to invest money in schemes which buy shares in chemical companies, the adviser must recommend schemes which exclude this sector of industry.

However, while the advisers are required to fully investigate the *financial* circumstances of their clients in order find suitable investments, there is no legal requirement on them to ask specifically if the investor has any *ethical* concerns. Within the regulations, it is left to the client to use their initiative to raise the ethical concerns – usually after an extensive interview in which searching questions are asked about their financial affairs.

This is clearly unsatisfactory since it is unclear how advisers could be satisfied they have all the necessary information unless they have asked if the investor has ethical concerns. As far as is known no investor has yet attempted to sue an adviser for giving poor advice on ethical issues, or not asking about them at all.

Professional advisers have access to computer networks giving up-to-the-minute summaries of the performance of different funds, and potential investors should ask to see these comparisons. Advisers are also required to declare the commissions they will earn when placing business with the financial institutions. Although the commissions have to be described in a standard form, prospective investors should ask to see commission statements for a range of different companies before deciding.

Most investment opportunities are explained in the financial services jargon which outsiders find difficult to understand: advisers should explain how the contracts work *in a way individual investors can understand.* If your adviser doesn't explain the contracts so you understand them, find another adviser.

A full list of advisers giving ethical advice is included in the appendix. EIRIS (see Chapter 6) will give details of what proportion of each adviser's work is in the ethical sector – it is better to go to an adviser who does more than dabble in the subject.

Barchester Green Investment

Giles Chitty of Barchester was involved in promoting green investment even before the the launch of the longest running ethical unit trust – Friends Provident's Stewardship.

Barchester say they undertake more ethical and investment business than any of the specialist independent financial advisers in the UK, and 'receive inquiries from all over the world, from the European Space Centre to Outer Mongolia'.

They do not, however, only deal with green and ethical investments: 'Barchester will never ask you to commit yourself to investing on a 100% ethical basis before advising you on the practical and financial implications. We believe such an approach to be highly questionable.

'Many areas of financial services do not have a green option', they say,

'There are also some "grey" areas which can be covered by "green" policies, but the option is not always a satisfactory one and we believe the risks of "going green" – where risks exist – should be clearly pointed out to prospective clients before they make their decision'.

Most clients of Barchester nevertheless choose the ethical options – and in early 1996 only 15% of their business did not meet these criteria.

Barchester run their own fund called 'Best of Green' which is managed by the ethical stockbroker A.E. Sharp & Co. They also run the Barchester Green and Ethical Unit Trust Portfolio which is a 'fund of funds' (see Chapter 7) which invests in other ethical unit trusts (to spread risk further but with the disadvantage of higher charges).

The Ethical Investors Group

Lee Coates of the Ethical Investors Group will *only* advise on ethical investments, and stresses that where an adviser or institution runs ethical and non-ethical contracts in parallel, the influence of the former is greatly diluted.

'If I state that I will only invest some of my clients' money in a company if certain green standards are adopted, the influence of this is much reduced if the company knows that I will still be putting non-ethical money their way', says Lee.

He could add that while many ethical investors wish to avoid companies because particular departments are undertaking activities they don't agree with, they are equally likely to want to avoid an adviser whose other work involves placing money with any company regardless of its ethical standards.

The Ethical Investors Group states:

Socially responsible investment allows individuals and companies to invest in a responsible way, without compromising their beliefs and principles. If enough people follow this investment path, it is hoped that companies will eventually be forced to review their strategy and become more socially responsible, or face possible reductions in their share prices and consequently a loss of confidence in the company.

EIG also pledges to donate half its profits each year to causes nominated by its clients, and in the company's first six years they gave away a total of £121,000 to some 159 groups and charities.

According to Lee Coates, EIG 'actively campaigns for companies to adopt environmentally and socially responsible policies...and are the acknowledged pioneers of cruelty-free investment in the UK'.

Davies & Chapman

Davies and Chapman specialises in providing financial advice to women. Partner Julia Davies says much of the financial services industry is 'fairly chauvinistic in attitude' and she says 'women are more resistant to the hard sell and have a greater degree of scepticism'. She says 90 per cent of their clients want to invest ethically, but after discussions, only about 60 per cent actually do so.

Like most advisers, Davies and Chapman does not undertake investment directly into companies: they funnel their clients cash through funds, and also don't advise investing in the 'social economy'.

To remove the incentive of selling investments which earn high commissions, the partnership will offer a flat rate charge regime. 'This is to remove the sense of prospecting for sales', says Julia. 'It is uncomfortable if all the work is done and the only way to be paid is by selling investments which earn us commission'.

'We sell our service and the idea of financial planning. We give people information and help them make their own decisions. It is education and counselling'.

Holden Meehan

Holdan Meehan are probably the UK's largest ethical financial advisers in terms of amounts invested. They say:

> There are now a number of independent advisers providing advice on these (ethical and green) funds. Most follow Holden Meehan's lead which is to recommend alongside ethical products, conventional ones such as national savings, government securities, and with-profits savings products where appropriate from a financial planning perspective. Our view is that until the ethical market can fill this gap, serious consideration should be given to putting financial security before a purist green approach.
> Most of the people approaching us for advice have already bought financial arrangements that are not ethically screened. Rather than re-arranging their existing plans our approach is that of building onto the existing portfolio. Even when making recommendations from scratch, for example for someone who wants to invest a lump sum, we may still advise a mixed approach. Ethical funds which are based on stock market investments may only provide a part of the solution. There are advisers who take a different view on this, but they are in the minority, and their perspective can be established over the telephone before a meeting.

In practice what this means, according to Holden Meehan partner Philip Chapman, is: 'We don't really get involved in talking about individual companies. Our concern is to fully check the ethical criterion and back-up research of a fund in the first place. People buying into a fund know they are buying an off-the-shelf product and they take a pragmatic view'. (Holden Meehan, do, however, look at companies when making up specific packages for people with over £100,000 to invest.)

Like all financial advisers, Holden Meehan will first ask a new client a range of questions about their financial status before making any recommendations. One question is headed 'Ethical or environmental concerns – areas of investment to be avoided or specifically aimed at', and the client has the opportunity to raise issues they wish to. Clients are *not* given a list of ethical concerns (like those in Chapters 4 and 5 above, or the list published by EIRIS – see Chapter 6).

'Giving people a long list may just make people throw up their hands and say it's not worth finding ethical and green investments', says Philip Chapman. 'We want to hear their thoughts and not impose or influence them with ours'.

Holden Meehan publish a 20 page 'Independent Guide to Ethical and Green Investment Funds' which states that:

Our view, based on the evidence, is that it is possible to achieve above average performance in the medium to long term by investing in ethical funds. Certainly we do not believe that an investor will be disadvantaged by investing in a socially responsible manner.

Ethical investment has moved from the fringe to the mainstream and it's there to stay. Even if we accept that the moral principles which guide other aspects of our lives have no place in our financial affairs – there are still sound reasons for including at least some screened funds in a portfolio. As international directives on pollution and working practices come into force, those companies which are out of line will find themselves out of pocket too, facing severe financial penalties.

11

Active shareholding

• •

> 'The business of business is to keep the company alive and breath-
> lessly excited, to protect the workforce, to be a force for good in our
> society and then, after all that, to think of the speculators. I have never
> kow-towed to the speculators or considered them to be my first respon-
> sibility. They play the markets without much concern for the company
> or its values. Most are only interested in the short-term and quick
> profit; they don't come to our Annual General Meetings and they don't
> respond to our communications. As far as I am concerned
> I have no obligations to these people at all'.
>
> Anita Roddick, *Body and Soul*, 1992

MOST INVESTORS ARE content to deposit their money and wait – and
hope – for the profits to roll in. Ethical investors will also want the
company or bank to perform to a particular standard, and will sell shares or
withdraw cash if those standards aren't met.

Such attitudes effectively allows company directors and investment
managers a free rein to behave as they wish, subject only to limited regulations which might curb their greatest excesses.

Yet shareholders in theory 'own' the company and thus have a right to
influence how it performs. To all intents and purposes these rights have
almost become defunct: only a tiny minority of shareholders exercise any
control over companies, and they bring only very little influence to bear to
get companies to improve their ethical standards. Conversely company directors have come to believe and act as though they own the company. In a few
companies, they do, but in most, the ownership rests with the outside shareholders. To many observers, it seems the only time the individual
shareholders matter is when their approval is being sought for a takeover bid.

There are a handful of pressure groups which have bought shares so that
their activists can attend annual general meetings of particular companies,
and a group of institutional investors have attempted to exert influence, but
in the main directors do as they wish.

This is a pity, since of all the stakeholders in a business – shareholders, employees, customers, suppliers, creditors, and the local community – it is only shareholders who have the right to meet with the directors and question them in a quasi-public forum: the annual general meeting.

Companies are required by law to hold AGMs, and attendance is normally restricted to directors, shareholders and their proxies, and the press. Significantly, the people whose work keeps the company running – the employees – have no right to attend.

Shareholders have the right at the AGM to table resolutions, elect the directors, and ask questions. Thus investors wanting to promote ethics and green standards in companies have an almost unique opportunity through share ownership to directly give their views to people running the company.

Shareholder rights

Shareholders in listed companies have the following legal rights:
1. To attend shareholders' meetings.
2. To bring resolutions before the meetings.
3. To vote on the appointment of directors.
4. To vote on the appointment of auditors.
5. To approve the directors' report and accounts.
6. To vote on any other resolutions put to the meetings.
7. To ask questions of the directors.

To the companies, annual meetings are crucial public relations events: they are a regular opportunity to show the financial world that the company is well run and producing impressive profits and dividends. Such an impression can help maintain the share price and secure the company's future borrowing requirements. The presence of the press means directors need to be on their best behaviour – photographs of security staff forcibly removing shareholders does not promote the image of a caring and responsible company.

Nevertheless, while shareholders have legal rights to participate in the AGM, these rights are hedged around with restrictions. (There have been proposals from the government to change these regulations, but in mid 1996 there was considerable uncertainty as to whether this would actually happen and whether the changes would give more power to shareholders, or remove it from campaigners and activists.)

Attending the AGM

All shareholders – no matter the size of their holding – are entitled to attend the AGM. Individual shareholders unable to attend can nominate a proxy on their behalf: they don't need to be owners of shares in their own right.

Proposing a resolution

The biggest restriction on shareholder action is the rules governing the placing of a resolution on the AGM agenda.

Firstly, resolutions must be proposed either by owners of at least 5% of the voting shares, or by 100 shareholders who each paid an average of £100 for their shares. The former requirement is likely to mean shareholders holding millions of pounds of shares so the latter is likely to be the only viable option. (Lists of shareholders are available from the company itself or Companies House.)

Secondly, resolutions must be filed with the company in sufficient time for them to be distributed to shareholders and proxies with the other papers for the meeting. However companies do not normally announce the actual date of the AGM until a few weeks beforehand, thus making it very difficult to dovetail the two dates (particularly since the company is unlikely to have ever received an independent shareholders' resolution before, and will almost certainly not welcome it).

Thirdly, the law requires the proposers of a resolution to pay the costs of circulating it to shareholders. If the resolution has been submitted before the proxy forms are printed the extra costs should be the extra space the resolution and accompanying statement take up. This could be 'just' a few hundred pounds, but if a special mailing is required for all shareholders, and this could be hundreds of thousands of recipients, the costs could be many thousands of pounds.

These are minimum conditions, and some companies have articles in their memorandum of association which further restrict the activities of shareholders – for instance a ban on resolutions covering 'operational matters' which could be deemed to be the exclusive province of the directors.

Voting on a resolution

Most resolutions are simply put to a vote at the AGM with shareholders raising their hands. This procedure is followed for the uncontroversial resolutions put by the directors (such as re-appointment of the auditors) and can give the mistaken impression of great democracy; here apparently the number of shares doesn't matter, and everyone has one vote no matter the shareholding. The practice dates back to the early days of limited companies when it was believed shareholders should enjoy some equality among themselves. However, the shareholders or the directors can ask for a poll in which case votes are taken according to the number of shares held – and this procedure is likely to be invoked if a controversial resolution has been passed on a show of hands. Proxies are not allowed to vote on a show of hands – they can only register a vote in a poll. The directors themselves are usually nominated as proxies by most shareholders, and consequently the results of votes are generally known to directors before the meeting even begins.

Asking questions

The principal opportunity to put views over to company directors is by asking questions. Questions can be asked by any shareholders, irrespective of the size of their holding. Since most AGMs are uncontroversial, most questions will be answered courteously, but the directors will be very aware that views put at the meeting are likely to be minority views, and should matters be put to a vote, the result will go their way.

As some shareholders and pressure groups have begun to use AGMs to put public pressure on companies, directors have adopted some subtle procedures to exert control of the AGM. Some companies will direct investors who hold single shares to sit together – possibly even corralled in by security staff. The chair of the meeting can then try not to call anyone sitting in that block.

In the 1995 AGM of the company BET, the director somewhat snidely pointed out that a questioner only owned about ten shares, the implication to the meeting clearly being that such a small investment meant the questioner had little right to call the directors to task.

Other companies attempt to reduce the effectiveness of questions by controlling the sound system, so questioners seen as troublemakers are seated where they don't get the opportunity to speak through a microphone.

These tactics don't go down well with many shareholders, and even the UK Shareholders Association which looks somewhat askance at environmental campaigners commented: 'On arrival [at the Costain AGM] shareholders were submitted to an ordeal of writing out their names and address, followed by a body search – leading to long queues and some irritation. Once inside, burly guards were well-positioned in the seating. During questions some shareholders expressed annoyance at being treated 'like animals''. At the AGM of the company Signet, the Association commented: 'A problem expressed by some shareholders is losing the microphone (or finding the electricity has been turned off) when one wants to return comments. The first rule is *never* to let go of the microphone, which is often encouraged. Second, demand loudly for the current to be restored. Third, take up any unanswered matters with journalists present if directors don't (or won't) answer satisfactorily'.

Such company chicanery can be countered by purchasing more than a single share, by dressing smartly so as to be inconspicuous, by holding onto a microphone once you have asked your question, thus being able to put a follow-up, and sitting apart from friends in the hall.

Some organised groups, such as the Campaign Against the Arms Trade, have adopted much more pro-active stances at AGMs and have positively sought to disrupt the meetings. If you believe the company can be persuaded to change its stance through persuasion and reason, such disruption is likely to make your job more difficult. If you believe that a large company is basically ruthless and will pursue profits at all costs, then a demonstration at an AGM can focus media attention on a company and up the pressure.

These rights to influence the company you own (in partnership with others) may seem limited. Yet the rights are far greater than those enjoyed by the other stakeholders, or by investors in unit trusts, pensions, PEPs, and life assurance schemes. These investments give the saver no legal opportunity to influence how their money is being used.

Investment in unit trusts does not confer the right to attend the AGMs of the companies in which the investments are held, and nor do the unit trusts normally themselves hold meetings for investors.

Recent changes to record keeping of stocks and shares have led stockbrokers to offer nominee accounts which allow shares to be quickly bought and sold. These accounts also mean the investor has no right to attend the company AGMs.

Hence the major shareholders in British industry – the financial institutions which own over 60% of company shares – have no direct pressure brought to bear on them by ethical investors. The only pressure is that caused indirectly by investors buying into ethical funds rather than mainstream ones. Within the institutions some managers actually want unitholders and purchasers of pensions to bring pressure to bear: the manager of one large ethical fund said he found it very disappointing that he receives only a handful of letters a year from investors. He says he replies in detail as to why particular investments are chosen, but generally receives no other communication back. He confesses to becoming disheartened and wishes that clients would make their views known more forcefully.

This lack of pressure strengthens the argument of most mainstream fund managers that their responsibility is only to obtain the highest profit at the lowest risk from their investments. Many managers even claim that they are debarred by law from considering ethical issues.

However, if mainstream financial institutions were to be put under intense pressure by ethical investors, *they wouldn't be able to simply sell their shares in unacceptable companies and buy into ethical ones instead. The reason is that there simply aren't enough of the latter (whatever the criteria) to soak up the huge sums the institutions have to invest.*

If the institutions tried to sell large swathes of shares in unacceptable companies, many financial analysts predict the effect would be for those shares to slump in price, and possibly for the whole stock market to decline drastically.

Hence financial institutions coming under pressure from ethical investors are likely to be forced to play a more active role in changing the way companies operate. They might have to tell companies to change their means of operation so that certain ethical standards are met.

This is the scenario Pensions Investments Research Consultants (PIRC) wants to see. PIRC campaigns to persuade the financial institutions to become active shareholders.

The institutions are unlikely to take up this position until they believe their investors want them to. Thus if you have a mainstream pension plan, life assurance, a PEP, unit trusts or an annuity, you hold a special responsibility to persuade them to take up ethical issues.

Some of the institutions hold meetings of their investors and these provide opportunities to ask questions and put views across. All institutions claim to take careful notice of letters sent in by investors.

While there are small organisations representing company shareholders (The UK Shareholders' Association) and building society members (The Building Society Members' Association), as far as is known there are no groups representing people who invest in unit trusts and pension funds. There is thus a serious 'gap in the market' for a campaigner to take up the cudgels on behalf of investors to persuade the funds to take on ethical issues.

Outside the law

Yorkshire Water was the company which was the target of what is believed to be the first successful shareholder resolution at a UK AGM.

The proposal was significant for two reasons. Firstly for its sheer lack of controversy: it read, 'Shareholders demand that the company ceases to commit unlawful acts'. Secondly, it nevertheless attracted a staggering 700,000 proxy votes opposed to it!

According to Stuart Bell of Pensions and Investment Research Consultants: 'The weird thing was that there were actually any votes against. It is hard to guess what these individuals and institutions were trying to say – that the company should commit unlawful acts?'

12

Spending as an investment

●●●

'I reflected on how companionship depends on what we have in our
heads and not on what we have in our pockets'.
John Stewart Collis, *The Worm Forgives the Plough*, 1946.

M OST OF US divide our money into the sums we need to spend each
week on day-to-day living and the amounts remaining which become
our savings and which we invest in one way or another.

Many of us also gain a comforting glow of satisfaction when we can justify
buying something as an investment. Such justification somehow excuses
what we might otherwise view as an extravagance. Nevertheless, many
purchases can and should be justified on the basis that there are sound financial and ethical reasons for making them.

Goods on sale can be roughly divided into three categories: items which
cease to have any value or use at all after they have been bought and used –
food is the best example; items which reduce in value once they become
secondhand – most furniture and cars; and items which retain their value or
appreciate over time such as antiques and (usually) property.

In addition some purchases can have an ethical benefit which can mean it
is better to spend your money on them rather than depositing it in an ethical
bank. Investments are usually viewed as a way of using money which allows
you to recover the money in the future, preferably with some financial profit.

For the ethical investor the benefit and 'profit' are not measured in purely
financial terms. And when investors start adding in all the non-financial
benefits of using money constructively, the advantages of ethical investment
can be wide ranging indeed.

There is growing evidence that spending money on organic food, for
example, can keep you healthier, thus allowing you to gain more from life,
and possibly to keep active for longer, thus reducing your reliance on benefits in the future. Buying a bicycle (and using it regularly) may have similar
benefits.

Buying goods from a local grocery store rather than a large supermarket
is likely to keep the store in business. This could mean that in the future you

will not be forced to travel further when the local shop closes – which could be when you are older, can't drive, and there are poor public transport services to the shops which have remained in business far away.

Other purchases could save money more directly and benefit the environment. Investing in insulation can reduce heat loss from your home resulting in less energy being required to keep it warm, and thus less greenhouse gases or nuclear radiation being emitted, as well as lower fuel bills.

Buying goods of high quality can also be a wise investment. Surveys of many consumer goods indicate the average life for many household goods and appliances is becoming shorter. Many manufacturing companies are trying to achieve two aims with their goods: they want customers to believe their product will last a long time – but they also want you to buy replacements at regular intervals. The influence of manufacturers (and fashion) is such that we barely question why many white goods (fridges, freezers, cookers, microwaves etc.) last only a few short years, while cars last on average about 11 years, and houses many decades or more. From a financial and environmental view buying products which last is likely to be a better use of money: good quality stainless steel saucepans carry guarantees of 25 years or more, compared with low quality and low cost aluminium pans which have been linked with the brain condition, Alzheimer's disease.

Virtually all day-to-day purchases can be looked at from an ethical or green perspective, while some purchases can be justified as a more attractive way of using money than keeping it in the bank, or buying unit trusts or company shares.

Alternative energy

Most of us accept the routine of having to pay the quarterly fuel bills. Fitting insulation (see below) and keeping lights switched off can save something on those bills, while investing in photovoltaic panels and windchargers can reduce electricity bills more substantially. Installing composting toilets and rainwater harvesting systems can reduce water costs. Solar panels to heat water can reduce electricity or gas bills.

These opportunities are often greater for rural dwellers than for those in towns and cities, and there are undoubtedly high capital costs to be paid before financial benefits start accruing. These capital costs – totalling several thousands of pounds if you want to generate electricity comparable to the mains supply, and perhaps £1500 for solar panels to heat water – mean many are discouraged from investing in this area.

The pressure to reduce greenhouse gas emissions and other pollutants, together with future scarcity of raw materials, is likely to mean that generating heat or electricity from the sun and wind will become more financially attractive. Many people believe with considerable justification that unless there is a wholesale switch to such environmentally benign energy systems, the planet will become so polluted that we will be forced to abandon our profligate ways of using and producing energy.

According to the Department of the Environment, investing in some energy saving measures in the home can bring returns far in excess of those available through the mainstream financial markets. The Department suggests, for example, that while lagging a hot water tank costs between £5 and £10, it produces financial savings of between £10 and £15 per year; while low energy light bulbs cost £5 to £15 and produce annual savings of £10. Draught excluder can cost, they suggest, between £45 and £60 and produce savings of £10 to £20 per year. These all produce considerable reductions of the greenhouse gas CO_2, as well as impressive financial savings.

Clothing

The slavish followers of fashion may be getting a lot of pleasure from dressing in the latest styles, but their bank balance and the environment will be suffering as a result.

Much clothing is now shipped many miles before appearing in your high street fashion stores, and some from Third World countries is made by children and adults (principally women) working very long hours. Clothes made from artificial fibres can have high energy costs.

The financial lesson is well learnt by inspecting the wardrobe of a fashion addict: rails of expensive clothes worn just a few times and then discarded.

A responsible investor would buy clothes made in the UK from natural fibres and wear them as long as possible.

Food

Most people's food buying has been taken over by the supermarkets which in the main sell products which are extensively packaged, with a wide range of chemical additives, and little regional variation.

Suppliers of goods to supermarkets – particularly small businesses – increasingly feel they have little power in the relationship, and see their food-stuffs travelling many miles before being put on sale.

The onward march of supermarkets has led to a drastic reduction in the number of 'ordinary' food shops, while the bulk buying power of supermarkets and adulteration of food makes it difficult to sell organic produce. Barely a month goes by without a new foodstuff or additive being exposed as a product hardly worth buying: eggs with salmonella, 'recycled' milk, beef from diseased cattle, carrots with excessive pesticide residues, bread with chalk dust added. These are all basic foodstuffs and wise investors would be well advised to divert some of their income to paying the premiums necessary to secure organic food. The benefits are likely to be better health, but, indirectly, financially advantageous too. The latter benefits may come in such areas as water bills, as customers meet the expenses of the water companies which are paying the high costs of treatment to remove excessive nitrates running off land not farmed organically.

The Soil Association is promoting a variety of ways of bringing organic food from grower to table, including various subscription systems. Some of these operate as virtually the only example of an ethical 'futures market' where buyers subscribe the cost of seed, labour and other overheads at the beginning of the growing seasons: this gives them a right to a share of the produce come harvest time. They thus invest in the farmer, and share in a bountiful crop (or suffer during a lean year). Such arrangements – and the subscription systems have a number of variants – bring together the grower and the customer so both understand each other's needs. Often the schemes encourage customers to spend some time working or visiting the farms.

The LETS alternative

If the problems of investing money ethically seem insurmountable, you could consider investing without using conventional money.

Local Exchange Trading Systems (LETS) are trading groups set up by communities to exchange goods and services without using government-issued money.

Members list their offers and wants in a directory and price them in terms of a local LETS currency. They record the transactions using cheques and one of the members periodically issues statements showing balances. Members can buy even when they don't have any LETS credits: they create the currency to pay for the transaction – a right much envied by those confined to the world of conventional money. Minus balances indicate members have committed themselves to undertaking some LETS work on the system to that value in the future. No interest is paid on plus or minus balances.

LETS systems are growing in the UK and elsewhere, but they are still small. Working on a LETS scheme could be an investment in the future of strong local communities since, in addition to the trading, the systems create strong community bonds.

Housing

Buying a house or flat is often regarded in the UK as a person's greatest investment. Until recently it was regarded as virtual foolishness to rent your home rather than buying it. Many misguided people paid more attention to the potential for profit from a house than to whether they themselves would enjoy living in it. This view took a knock in the early 1990s as the price of houses stabilised and in many cases declined and the phrase 'safe as houses' gained a very hollow ring indeed for some.

In most countries of the world, housing is not viewed as an investment at all: people are able to rent their homes for many years for moderate sums.

The ethical issues surrounding home ownership chiefly come down to a view as to whether it is right to gain financially from your home, since a case can be made that housing is a 'basic human right' and it is simply wrong to profit from it when many people are unable to secure decent accommodation.

Some would counter that it makes little difference whether the occupant owns or rents the house or flat: it is still occupied and not available for someone in greater need! There are grave ethical problems for a society where house prices are rising ever higher in a dizzying spiral, since this is what makes housing unobtainable for so many people. Indeed surveys show that there is no countrywide shortage of housing as such, the shortage is one of income to allow poorer people to buy or rent. Thus, there are many empty houses which are virtually unsaleable in areas where there are few jobs, and a shortage of homes in areas where work is available.

The difficulty for ethical investors when looking at house price inflation revolves around the theoretical issue of whether the inflation matches the cost of borrowing money on a mortgage. A mortgage can cost the borrower 10% per year over 25 years – that is, the purchaser actually ends up paying two and a half times the amount borrowed. So for the house value to match the mortgage, the value of the house has to increase by up to 10% per year.

More pertinently, investors need to consider who it is ethical to borrow money from to buy housing. Most of this book warns investors to see whether those to whom their money is lent are using it ethically. In the case of mortgages, the question is whether the lending institution – which is making the profit from you through the interest charged – uses that profit in an ethically sound way.

If you borrow from a building society, your money is likely to go towards paying interest on savings accounts held by private individuals – and unless you are going to question how they spend it, this is as satisfied as you can be. If you borrow from a bank, an insurance company, or through some sort of endowment or pension mortgage arrangement, the question is: where does the institution invest its money? Banks won't tell you who their customers are (see Chapter 8) and hence who they lend to, while there are ethical endowment and pension mortgages.

There are, however, powerful environmental reasons for purchasing your home rather than renting it. Many environmental improvements are more likely to be carried out by owners than tenants: installing insulation, solar panels, gas condensing boilers, conservatories to generate passive heat, and a wide range of other ideas simply aren't worth considering unless you have long term security.

Insurance

For most people insurance is a comparatively minor purchase. Yet insurance companies are now major players in the economy, and are likely to become a formative influence on how industry treats the environment.

Insurance companies hold the premiums they are paid by their customers until claims are made. In the meantime, the money is invested to gain the highest profits. It is estimated that the small number of insurance companies own a massive 16.5% of British industry, making them potentially very influential indeed. It is to the insurance companies that businesses look when claims for environmental damage have to be met, and this is making the underwriters look increasingly carefully at pollution issues.

It is estimated that the total potential damages claims from asbestosis victims and for cleaning up contaminated land in the United States come to more than the insurance industry's total assets. It is also estimated that a hurricane which tore through the southern US would have brought widespread bankruptcies among insurance companies if it had hit a major city just a few miles further north.

The touchiness of one insurer was revealed in early 1995 when a company in Worcestershire abruptly shut an incinerator emitting high levels of dioxins after it was warned by solicitors to advise its insurers that damages claims could be forthcoming from neighbours if it continued operating.

Such matters go to the heart of modern insurance: the policies are the only products sold in the marketplace where the supplier hopes they won't have to supply the service (the payout in the event of a claim).

Hence there are financial and environmental reasons for attempting to seek out ethical insurers. Unfortunately the choice is small: the Ethical Investors Group and Naturesave arrange insurance policies which take environmental issues into account to a very limited extent. Naturesave say they are the 'only buildings and contents insurance protecting you and the environment' and their aim is 'to encourage the adoption of more environmentally aware trading practices in the business community'. They give 10% of their premiums to environmental organisations, and those which have benefited include the Wiltshire Wildlife Trust and the Centre for Alternative Technology.

However the company won't say how much they have given to the organisations, and the other 90% of the premiums are invested through Lloyds underwriters – that is, the same way any insurance company will invest without taking ethical issues into account.

The Ethical Investors Group will arrange policies with insurance companies whose *working practices* have been screened by *The Ethical Consumer*, but who still invest their premium income without ethical considerations.

In late 1995 nearly 60 of the world's insurance companies supported a 'Statement of Environmental Commitment' which said: 'The insurance industry recognises that economic development needs to be compatible with human welfare and a healthy environment. To ignore this is to risk increasing social, environmental and financial costs. Our industry plays an important role in managing and reducing environmental risk. We are committed to work together to address key issues such as pollution reduction, the efficient use of resources, and climate change. We endeavour to identify realistic sustainable solutions'.

Despite this 'commitment' there is not a single insurance company in the UK offering general insurance policies where the premium income is invested with ethical considerations. Regardless of the high financial risk of insuring industries with a poor environmental record, insurers have hardly looked at the long term environmental issues with any sophistication.

You may however wish to insure with Co-operative Insurance Society (on the grounds that it is wholly owned by the retail Co-operative movement) or with Ecclesiastical (who also provide motoring, buildings, home contents and other insurance) if you like the fact that their profits go to the Church of England and to charities.

Woodland

Most woodland sold for investment in the UK consists of large tracts of monocrop planted for clearfelling. Such woods provide scant habitats for wildlife and leave a wake of devastation behind them when felled.

However, buying broadleaved, mixed woodland can bring long term financial returns as well as opportunities for low environmental impact work and leisure activities. A well managed woodland, in addition to keeping its price, can provide employment opportunities for those involved in the rapidly expanding coppicing industry as well as firewood, charcoal and timber sales. Some landowners refer to immature trees as their pensions, knowing that proper management will allow trees to be selectively cut in future years.

Clissett Wood in Herefordshire is a small mixed wood bought by a group of people interested in woodland crafts who each invested £5000. They use the wood in different ways. Some run green woodworking courses, others take wood for firewood and crafts. Others use it to retreat to from the world.

However, while the environmental benefit of such investment is strong, woods need proper management for both ecological and financial reasons.

13

Conclusion

● ●

H OW ETHICAL? How much will my investments earn? How much risk am I taking? These are the three questions which need to be upper-most in your mind when deciding where to place your money.

The professionals in the ethical fund world say that investing with them will not hurt your pocket. The view is based on the performance of the funds which invest in the stock market, many of which have been returning profits comparable to those from non-ethical funds. It is also based on the (unspoken) belief that investors simply won't take ethical considerations into account unless they receive a return comparable to that from non-ethical investments. If you as an investor will *only* accept this comparable return, you may not actually be helping ethical businesses in the long run. This is simply because much of the profit from stock market investments is from unsus-tainable economic activities which are harmful to the earth and its people. Put simply, expecting maximum return from, say, investing in land would entail building office blocks or expensive housing, or promoting intensive farming. Organic agriculture, social housing and managed workspaces for the unemployed won't give you comparable financial returns.

However the range of ethical investments extends far beyond the stock market institutions, and the returns can vary greatly. Put simply, in the short term, the more ethical you want to be with your savings, the lower will be the financial return, and the higher will be your contribution to improving the crazy world we all live in. In the longer term the less ethical you are, the greater the risk that the whole financial edifice will crumble: for the bottom line is that the economy rests on how well we look after the earth, the soil, the air and the water.

On an ethical scale, the majority of stock market companies and the funds which invest in them are at one extreme: many of them are doing serious damage to people, the planet and other species.

In the middle are the ethical unit trusts, bravely trying to separate the not-quite-so-bad stock market companies from the others. Also here is the Co-operative Bank with a set of ethical criteria based on a survey of customers' views.

At the opposite end of the scale, in the truly committed 'real' ethical world, are the social bank Triodos, and the Ecology Building Society, both of which will only deal with projects of environmental and social worth.

Also here are businesses such as Traidcraft and the Centre for Alternative Technology, and funds such as Radical Routes and the Aston Reinvestment Trust, which form the 'social economy'. Here the organisations see the service or products they supply and their relationship to the environment, the workers, the local community and customers as being more important than profit.

Many environmentalists and advocates of social change believe that the only route to a sustainable society is via the latter sector. Here, too, are to be found some of the most imaginative and radical ideas for finding new ways of using money in ethical ways.

These new ideas are desperately needed to counterbalance the huge sums of money which chase around the world seeking profit from investing in money – rather than from the exchange of goods and services. This continuous search for the highest return means that businesses and projects needing money are often forced to borrow at higher rates than necessary – making the products they are trading and producing more expensive than need be.

Within the financial world, many seem to have forgotten that money evolved to allow us to trade the things we need. Within businesses it seems to be forgotten that our planet's resources can provide for all our needs and comforts, but not for a profligate lifestyle which is undermining our very existence.

If you cannot resolve the conflict between risk/return and ethics, the best answer is: spread your money in different places, with some of it in the (better) funds where it is aiming to achieve growth comparable with non-ethical stock market investments.

But also place some in the ethical banks, and some in the social economy. And very importantly, put some into tangible assets such as land on which you can grow food, or tools with which you can make things people need – for if the economy crashes share certificates will be barely worth the paper they are written on.

Unlike mainstream investors you will gain two benefits: some profit, and the knowledge that your money is being used for social good. For it is when large numbers of people invest their money in this way that the ecologically unsound companies will realise they *have* to change, and the institutions will realise they *must* take ethics seriously.

Appendix 1

Green and ethical financial advisers

Financial advisers who offer advice on green and ethical investments and who are either members of the Green Independent Financial Advisers Association, or who undertake a substantial amount of this investment.

Adam Associates
19 St Augustines Street, Norwich, Norfolk NR3 3BY
01603 766975

Barchester Green Investment
Barchester House, 45/49 Catherine Street, Salisbury, Wilts. SP1 2DH
01722 331241

Bromige & Partners
22 Hartfield Road, Forest Row, East Sussex RH18 5DY
01342 826703

Chew Valley Financial Services
Woodlands, Chew Hill, Chew Magna, Bristol BS18 8SA
01275 333795

Contextual Financial Services
12 Copse Side, Farncombe, Godalming, Surrey GU7 1DH
01483 428844

Co-operative Bank Financial Advisers Ltd.
PO Box 101, 1 Balloon Street, Manchester M60 4EP
0161 834 6208

Coracle Financial Services Ltd.
Waverley House, 14 Exeter Drive, Wellington, Telford, Shropshire TF1 3PR
01952 245235

Crowe Money Advice
69 Jamestown Road, London NW1 7DB
0171 485 9738

Daniels Holt Investment Managers
Tunsgate Square, 98 High Street, Guildford, Surrey GU1 3QZ
01483 304183

Darley Insurance Consultants Ltd.
230 High Street, Bromley, Kent BR1 1PQ
0181 460 2000

David Walters Financial Services
Horseshoe Cottage, Brownbread Street, Ashburnham, E. Sussex TN33 9NX
01424 893113

Davies & Chapman
109-110 Bolsover Street, London W1P 7HF
0171 637 2793

Devonshire, Wilson & Co.
150/152 County Road South, Hull HU5 5NA
01482 565919

Earthwork Financial Planning
1-7 Princes Street, Albert Square, Manchester M2 4DQ
0161 839 3218

Ethical Financial
7-8 Ty Verion Business Park, Barry, South Glamorgan CF6 3BE
01446 421123

Ethical Financial Services
90 Maytree Crescent, North Watford, Herts WD2 6BW
01923 677971

Ethical Investors Group
Milestone, Greet Road, Greet, Cheltenham GL54 5BG
01242 604550

Fleming Associates
43 Brunswick Hill, Macclesfield, Cheshire SK10 1ET
01625 611791

Glavey & Co.
22 St Mary's Street, Wallingford, Oxon. OX10 OEW
01491 832278

Global & Ethical Investment Advice
13a Heaton Road, Withington, Manchester M20 4PX
0161 434 4681

Graham Scott Financial Planning
25 St Johns Hill, Shrewsbury, Shropshire SY1 1JJ
01743 245279

Holden Meehan
55 High Holborn, London WC1V 6DX
0171 404 6442

and
11th Floor, Clifton Heights, Bristol BS8 1EJ
0117 925 2874

Independent Insurance Consultants
53a Church Road, Gateley, Stockport SK8 4NG
0161 491 5199

The Investment Practice
10 Coombe Road, New Malden, Surrey KT3 4EE
0181 336 1044

Kingswood Consultants
29 North Street, Bicester, Oxon. OX6 7NB
01862 252545

Lupton Fawcett
Yorkshire House, Greek Street, Leeds LS1 5SX
0113 246 9696

Mayfield Mackenzie
1 Cannington, Newick Lane, Mayfield, East Sussex TN20 6RA
01435 872317

Nichols Williams Durrant & Co Ltd.
Devonshire House, Devonshire Avenue, Roundhay, Leeds LS8 1AY
0113 269 7744

Priory Investment Management
The Old Tannery, Oakdene Road, Redhill, Surrey RH1 6BT
01737 779939

Rainbow IFA
16 South Queen Street, Morley, Leeds LS27 9EW
0113 238 1993

Ross & Co Financial Services
3 St Andrews Court, Thame, Oxon. OX9 3WT
01844 261400

Shepherd Financial Independent Services
Shepherd House, Sutton Howgrave, nr. Bedale, North Yorks. DL8 2NN
0800 591 899

Southernhays
22 Southernhay West, Exeter, Devon EX1 1PR
01392 410080

Symon Ashley
The Chandlery, 50 Westminster Bridge Road, London SE1 7QY
0171 721 7618

Tree of Life Financial Services
14 Croftdown Road, Harborne, Birmingham B17 8RB
0121 427 8250

Trevor Allingham,
AC House, Collins Court, High Street, Cranleigh, Surrey GU6 8AS
01483 274898

Verdi, Bowker & Bowker
13-14 Park Place, Leeds LS1 2SJ
and
83 Fountain Street, Manchester M2 2EE
and
14 Corporation Street, Birmingham B2 4RN
0800 581634

Verblow Macleod Associates
Studio Crown Reach, 149a Grosvenor Road, London SW1V 3JY
0171 834 9474

J.D.Ward (Financial Services) Ltd.
9 Kingsway, London WC2B 6XF
0171 836 4321

Wise Investment
Cross Leys, Chipping Norton, Oxon OX7 5HG
01608 642233

Appendix 2

Green and ethical funds and investment trusts

Funds which invest in the stock market, and the ethical and/or green criteria adopted when investing. The criteria listed are as described in the funds' own brochures and are likely to change over time. Funds are included which adopt any non-financial criteria when investing – although some of these funds would not themselves claim to be part of the ethical or green investment world.

Abbey Life Ethical Trust

Abbey Life Investment Services Ltd., 100 Holdenhurst Road, Bournemouth BH8 8AL

01202 292373

'To be included companies must fall into one of the following categories:

- Health care: companies which actively provide solutions to human health problems and are at the forefront of science and technology in their fields;
- Care for the Elderly: companies whose main responsibility is the provision of quality healthcare to the sick and the elderly;
- Healthy Eating: companies which are directly involved in either the production or retailing of organic produce and innovative fresh foodstuffs;
- Good Working Practices and Customer Care: companies which take pride in good management of its staff i.e. decent conditions of employment and strong commitment to staff training and development, high service levels to customers and the general public are important considerations, together with facilities for and employment of disabled people;
- Quality Goods: companies which have a commendable track record of high quality products, with due regard for safety and positive action in complaints.
- Environmental Protection and Control: companies which are at the forefront of improving the state of the environment either through the provision of pollution control and recycling services and/or relevant high technology equipment.
- Safety and Security: companies whose business is to manufacture or provide services in the fields of safety and security.
- Emerging Countries Project: Companies which encourage projects with developing countries e.g 'trade not aid' together with encouragement of policies to replace natural materials used in manufacture, e.g tropical hardwoods.

• Education: companies which either provide education services to a high standard and/or publish educational books and magazines.

• Relaxation and Family Leisure: companies which help facilitate relaxation and family leisure either through the provision of services such as community radio, holidays or hobbies.

Areas strictly excluded from investment:
  • Alcohol and tobacco production.
  • Animal experimentation for cosmetics.
  • Armaments.
  • Exploitation of endangered species.
  • Gambling.
  • Nuclear processing.
  • Pornography.

Companies 'engaged in positive ethical activities but with a small involvement in areas which are not entirely satisfactory' will be included 'if the undesirable aspects do not account for more than 10 per cent of sales, profits or capital invested'.

These include the following categories:
  • Sale of alcohol products.
  • Sale of tobacco products.
  • Involvement with undemocratic regimes.
  • Exploitation of scarce resources'.

Abtrust Ethical Fund

Abtrust Unit Trust Managers Ltd., 10 Queens Terrace, Aberdeen AB9 1QJ
01224 633070

The fund 'actively seeks companies that make a positive contribution to the environment, including those tackling problems such as pollution, toxic waste, and ozone depletion from within the industries responsible for their creation.

Abtrust does not invest in companies which have:
• Significant alcohol production.
• Significant tobacco production.
• Nuclear power production capacity.
• Any armaments production or sales capacity.
• Any connection with gambling.
• Any connection with animal testing.
• Fur farming or production interests.
• Interests in pornography.
• Ozone depleting chemical manufacturing operations.
• Operations manufacturing or selling "banned" pesticides.
• Exceeded water pollution parameters repeatedly'.

Acorn Ethical Unit Trust

City Financial Unit Trust Managers, 1 White Hart Yard, London SE1 1NX
0171 407 5966

Companies excluded are those 'manufacturing or distributing arms and armaments, tobacco and alcoholic products and drugs; and companies participating in animal experiments for research and development for their products'.

Allchurches Amity Fund

Allchurches Investment Management Services Ltd., Brunswick Road, Gloucester GL1 1JZ
01452 305958

'The fund aims to invest in companies which demonstrate a positive contribution to the quality of individual and community life and which respect and protect the environment. The investment programme includes companies involved, for example, in pollution control, waste management, energy conservation, housing, education, home safety, medical and health care.

The principal areas which the trust seeks to avoid are companies with material interests in countries with repressive regimes, and in the alcohol, tobacco and gambling industries, manufacturers of armaments, and those who produce magazines or video tapes of an explicit or violent nature or in research where animals are experimented on for cosmetic purposes'.

Al Medina Equity Fund

Faldo Hassard & Co., 22 Crawford Place, London W1H 1JE
0171 724 9188

This company was contacted a number of times requesting details of their fund, but no information was provided.

Barchester Best of Green, Best of Green Offshore, Barchester Green Ethical Unit Trust Portfolio, and Minerva Green Ethical Portfolio

Barchester Green Investment, 45/49 Catherine Street, Salisbury, Wilts. SP1 2DH
01722 331241

The *Best of Green* and *Best of Green Offshore* funds' criteria are as follows:
'Pro-active Criteria
The fund managers will seek to invest in company groups which:
• are involved in recycling and/or disposal of waste in a responsible way.
• have a public environmental statement and/or have had an independent environmental audit in the last three years.
• sponsor conservation projects or use wind, wave or geothermal energy sources in the UK.
• have a public Equal Opportunities policy.
• manufacture or sell products or provide services whose purpose is to save or protect human life.

- train their own staff in safety techniques.
- are involved in training and educational products and services.
- derive more than 25 per cent of their annual turnover from the sale or manufacture of "basic necessities".
- include a part that is a member of the "Ten Per Cent Club", Business in the Community, or amongst the top 25 donors to charity.

Reactive Criteria

The fund will avoid investing in company groups which:

- have derived any turnover from the uranium fuel cycle, handle radioactive waste, or supply equipment services other than safety or security equipment.
- have been convicted by Her Majesty's Inspectorate of Pollution.
- manufacture pesticide products.
- are involved in the extraction or growing of commodities in the third world.
- import, process or merchant timber, unless tropical hardwood free.
- have been found not fully compliant with the International Code of Conduct on marketing breast milk substitutes in the third world.
- have infringed the International Code of Conduct on the distribution and use of pesticides in the third world since 1988.
- are banks and according to Christian Aid, were owed money by third world countries in the last financial year.
- are classified as major arms traders by the Campaign Against the Arms Trade.
- are involved in the sale of, or production of, weapons systems or related services.
- are involved in the sale or production of non-civilian goods for military users.
- have been involved in the construction or management of, or strategic services for, nuclear bases.
- are involved in the export of goods or services for military users or which have exhibited at defence equipment exhibitions.
- manufacture pharmaceuticals, medicines, vitamins, soaps or cosmetics unless they are animal-test-free.
- derive any turnover from poultry or pig-farming unless intensive methods are not used.
- include a significant subsidiary or associated company in a country where human rights violations place them on the EIRIS list.
- derive more than 10 per cent of their reported annual turnover from the production or sale of tobacco or tobacco related products.
- derive more than 10 per cent of their reported annual turnover from the production or sale of alcoholic drinks.
- derive more than 10 per cent of their reported annual turnover from gambling.
- which publish, print, or wholesale magazines that the Council Against Pornography and Censorship say contain material that falls within its proposed legal definition of pornography.

- distribute film or videos that have been cut to obtain an 18 certificate.
- give political donations in excess of £25,000 (except where the political party concerned is receiving a comparatively low level of donations from business)'.

The Barchester Green Ethical Unit Trust Portfolio invests in the following funds: Friends Provident Stewardship, Stewardship Income, and Stewardship North American; Jupiter Ecology; Clerical Medical Evergreen; Scottish Equitable Ethical; and NPI Global Care. The criteria will therefore be those adopted by these funds.

The Minerva Green Ethical Portfolio invests in the funds of Abbey Ethical, Allchurches Amity, Sovereign Ethical, CIS Environ and Credit Suisse Fellowship. Its criteria will therefore be those adopted by these funds.

CIS Environ Trust

CIS Unit Manager Ltd., PO Box 105, Manchester M4 8BB
0161 832 8686

'The general rule is that, in order to qualify, companies must be involved wholly or in part in the manufacture of products, industrial processes or the provision of services associated with improving the environment and the enhancement of human health and safety. In addition, companies may qualify if they promote awareness of these issues amongst the general public or are likely to be the beneficiaries, in the medium-to-long term, of changing attitudes in favour of a cleaner and safer environment. Consideration will also be given to companies seen to be making above-average efforts to minimise environmental damage caused by their activities. The Trust also invests in companies engaged in certain activities which are considered to improve the quality of life of the population in general or a specific section of the population. This can include areas such as medical, scientific and educational publishing, education and training, electricity distribution, and telecommunications in under-developed parts of the world.

Once a company has been selected on the basis of the positive criteria, it is screened to establish whether it is active in areas which the Trust seeks to avoid:

- Animal testing: companies which conduct tests on animals are avoided unless those tests are conducted for the benefit of human health or animal health. This is taken to include testing related to foodstuffs as well as that related to pharmaceutical products.
- Items with military applications: suppliers of goods and services which have predominantly military applications are avoided. This avoidance does not apply if the items in question also have civilian uses or if they are concerned primarily with health or safety.
- Companies are avoided which have a significant amount of business in countries considered to have oppressive regimes. The fund's advisory committee reviews regularly a list of such countries, which includes states considered to have exhibited substantial disregard for human rights. Consideration may be given to cases where the activity of the company could be regarded as being beneficial for the local population or where there has been a substantial change of circumstances.

- Tobacco: Companies concerned with the manufacture of tobacco and tobacco-related products are avoided. This avoidance does not extend to general retailing and distribution.
- Generation of nuclear power: Unless there are exceptional mitigating circumstances, investments in companies involved in the generation of nuclear power are avoided. This will normally mean a complete avoidance of companies supplying goods and services for the process of generating nuclear power. However, companies whose activities are considered to mitigate any possible harm resulting from the process, for instance by manufacturing safety equipment, decommissioning plants or searching for safer ways of using nuclear power, might be acceptable.

In no circumstances will investment be allowed in a company where over 10 per cent of turnover is derived from activities involving the areas of avoidance noted in the four first exclusions above, and in most cases the exposure to these areas will in practice be much less that 10 per cent. The avoidance under nuclear power is stricter, with no involvement at all other than in the circumstances specified'.

Clerical Medical Evergreen Trust
Clerical Medical Unit Trust Managers, Narrow Plain, Bristol, BS2 0JH
0117 955 4711

'Investments considered appropriate will typically have interests in one or more of the following areas:
- Air quality/emissions control.
- Drinking water purification.
- Energy conservation.
- Environmental assessment.
- Geothermal energy.
- Natural Gas.
- Pollution analysis.
- Recycling.
- Site remediation.
- Waste reduction/disposal.
- Waste water treatment.
- Windpower.

The fund manager will seek to avoid companies which are involved in:
- Production, sale or distribution of fur products.
- Production, sale, or distribution of cosmetics where animal testing may be involved.
- Manufacture of ozone depleting chemicals (CFCs and halons).
- Manufacture or distribution of harmful pesticides.
- Supply of tropical hardwoods.

- Production, processing or sale of meat products.
- Manufacture or provision of armaments.
- Companies involved in repressive regimes (as listed by EIRIS) to a total extent of 10 per cent of group turnover.
- Provision of gambling services.
- Production of tobacco products.
- Production or distribution of pornography'.

Credit Suisse Fellowship Trust

Credit Suisse Investment Funds (UK) Ltd., Beaufort House, 15 St Botolph Street, London EC3A 7JJ
0171 247 7474

'The fund will not invest in:
- Producers of alcoholic drinks or companies which derive more than 10 per cent of their reported annual turnover from the sale of alcoholic drinks.
- Companies which derive any turnover from gambling.
- Producers of tobacco or tobacco products and companies which derive more than 10 per cent of their reported annual turnover from the sale of tobacco or tobacco products.
- Companies which have been involved in the sale or production of weapons systems and producers of strategic goods or services for military users.
- Nuclear military activities.
- Companies which supply ozone depleting chemicals (ODCs) or engage in industrial activities often using ODCs unless products and processes are ODC-free.
- Companies which have received approval from MAFF or HSE to market pesticide products in the UK which include active ingredients that are banned or restricted in five or more countries.
- Companies with a poor track record on pollution.
- Companies which employ more than one per cent of their worldwide workforce in South Africa and have paid unacceptable wage rates in the last year, or fail to give enough information to assess wages in South Africa.

The fund will consider investing in:
- Companies with a consistently sound record on environmental and social issues.
- Substantial involvement in reducing overall waste through recycling, effective waste management or energy conservation.
- Companies who offer alternatives to animal tested goods, or use humane food production methods.
- Companies committed to a positive approach to social issues, particularly concerning their employees and the local community'.

CU Environmental Trust PLC

Commercial Union Investment Management Ltd., St Helen's, 1 Undershaft, London EC3P 3DQ
0171 662 6017

'The company's principal investment objective will be to invest in companies which either are, or will become, major beneficiaries of environmental protection expenditure. Potential investments in the environmental sector currently include companies engaged in activites as diverse as emission control systems, atmospheric monitoring, waste management and water treatment, as well as recycling, energy conservation, and water utilities'.

The Environmental Trust is a company listed on the Stock Exchange, not a unit trust.

Eagle Star Environmental Opportunities Trust

Eagle Star Unit Managers, Eagle Star House, Montpellier Drive, Cheltenham, Glos. GL53 7LQ
01242 577555

'The manager will normally invest in companies which are likely to benefit from their concern for the environment'. (No other information given.)

EIG Cruelty Free Fund

Ethical Investors Group, Milestone, Greet Road, Greet, Cheltenham GL54 5BG
01242 604550

'Positive criteria:
The Cruelty-Free Fund aims to encourage investment in areas such as:
• Alternative energy.
• Cruelty-free products.
• Energy conservation.
• Fair trade.
• Recycling.
• Ethical employment practices.
Exclusion criteria:
The Cruelty-Free Fund excludes investment in companies engaged in:
• Production, processing or sale of meat or dairy products.
• Production, processing or sale of animal-tested products.
• Environmental pollution.
• The arms trade.
• Oppressive regimes.
• Alcohol and tobacco production'.

The Environmental Investment Co.

Abacus Asset Management Ltd., La Motte Chambers, St. Helier, Jersey JE1 1BJ
01534 602000

The company invests in 'the securities of companies which should benefit from increased spending on environmental products and services. Environmental products and services are those which prevent, ameliorate, redress or measure damage to the natural environment'.

EIC is an investment trust listed on the Stock Exchange, not a unit trust.

Equitable Ethical Trust

Equitable Unit Trust Managers Ltd., Crown House, 51 Aldwych, London WC2B 4AX
0171 379 3000

'Investments will be made in companies operating in the following areas: pollution control, environmental protection, efficient utilisation of material and energy resources, clean fuels and alternative energy systems, and health care services and medical technology.

The trust will strive to avoid investments in companies involved in any of the following areas: alcohol, animal testing (including drug development), armaments, banking, fur trade, gambling, significantly associated with countries with undemocratic regimes, nuclear power production, polluting the environment (e.g CFCs and pesticides), pornography, and tobacco'.

Fidelity UK Growth Trust

Fidelity Investment Services Ltd., Oakhill House, 130 Tonbridge Road, Hildenborough, Kent TN11 9DZ
0800 414161

'The trust does not invest in the shares of tobacco or tobacco related companies'.

(This Trust does not claim to be an 'ethical fund' and bars tobacco-related investments because of an arrangement with the medical profession.)

Framlington Health Fund

Framlington Unit Managers Ltd., 155 Bishopsgate, London EC2M 3XJ
0171 374 4100

'The fund aims to invest in health care and medical services and product companies worldwide. The policy of the fund is to invest subject to ethical guidelines. Investment will be in producers of pharmaceuticals, bio-technology firms, medical device and instrument manufacturers, distributors of health care products, care providers and managers and other health care service companies.

The fund's emphasis is on companies that are providing innovative products or solutions for unmet medical needs. We regard this as adopting a positive ethical stance, although investors should be aware that pharmaceutical companies are required by law to test their products on animals before entering human clinical trials'.

Friends Provident Stewardship Unit Trust, Income Trust, North American Unit Trust, Life Fund, Individual Pension Fund

Friends Provident Life Office, United Kingdom House, 72-122 Castle Street, Salisbury SP1 3SH
01722 413366

'Those companies which demonstrate positively, by the conduct of their business, their suitability for inclusion are identified against the following criteria:

• Responsibility to the communities in which they operate, including the provision of products and services of long-term benefit to the community, e.g safety equipment.
• A record of suitability, quality and safety of products and services.
• Companies practising or involved in environmental improvement and pollution control.
• Conservation of natural resources including natural woodlands and forests, or energy conservation.
• The company's openness about its activities.
• The company's general approach to the management of its staff, customers and relationship with the public.

Companies which are involved in the following practices will normally be excluded from the portfolio:

• Companies whose activities are considered to degrade the environment including water pollution, associations with the provision of nuclear power, destruction of natural woodlands or forests, or the manufacture or distribution of ozone depleting chemicals, e.g CFCs or pesticides.
• Exploitation of animals, including the production of animal-tested cosmetics or products, sale of furs, intensive and factory farming related to the production and processing of meat.
• Companies with substantial trade or with subsidiary operations or associated interests in any country with an oppressive regime.
• Those companies with contracts of a military nature including manufacture or sale of military weapons or associated military uses, other than minor components or those satisfying basic personal needs.
• Activities resulting in repeated prosecutions by the Health and Safety Executive and the National Rivers Authority, or complaints upheld by the Advertising Standards Authority.
• Tobacco or alcohol production, and distribution of such products where this is a major part of their business.
• The production or distribution of material or films of a violent or pornographic nature.
• Companies involved in gambling.
• Financial institutions, a substantial part of whose loans and investments cannot be monitored.
• Companies involved in the unreasonable exploitation of people generally'.

Henderson Touche Remnant Ethical Fund

Henderson Unit Trust Managers Ltd., 3 Finsbury Avenue, London EC2M 2PA
0800 832832

'The fund will not invest in:

- Producers of alcohol or tobacco, or companies trading in or involved with gambling or pornography.
- Manufacturers of ozone depleting chemicals and companies seen to be taking insufficient action to stop using ozone depleting chemicals in their own products.
- Nuclear energy production, or manufacturers of equipment, other than for safety, which is needed in nuclear energy production.
- Tropical timber extraction or trading.
- Intensive farming.
- Producers of pesticides banned in more than five countries.
- Testing of products on animals – even for pharmaceuticals.
- Substantial economic presence (as defined by Dun & Bradstreet's 'Principal International Business' report) in a country where human rights have been abused (unless the company concerned has a positive record there according to the independent bodies monitoring these issues.)
- Nuclear military activities.
- Providers of goods or services vital to military operations, weapons manufacturers or the managers of a military base – this includes combat, communication and training equipment.
- Poor track record (e.g. repeated offences or fines according to conviction records received in the last three years) on any of the following: health and safety, employee relations and working conditions, advertising standards and pollution.
- Companies which exploit disparity around the world in employment regulations, environmental standards or safety procedures.

When the negative objectives are not contravened, the fund will consider investing in:

- Companies with a consistently sound record on environmental and social issues.
- Companies which aim to contribute in a positive way to society in general.
- Sustainable users of resources and companies who are improving their energy efficiency.
- Substantial involvement in reducing overall waste through recycling, effective waste management or energy conservation.
- Improving the standard of drinking water.
- Special attention to protecting rivers and seas.
- Traders of tropical timber that is sustainably grown or where the company has a policy for early phase out.
- Growers and sellers of produce that is not treated with synthetic pesticides.
- Companies who offer alternatives to animal tested goods, or use humane food production methods.

• Companies committed to a positive approach to a social issues, particularly concerning their employees and the local community.

• Companies with a high level of openness on all aspects of their business activities'.

Homeowners Green Chip Fund

Homeowners Friendly Society, PO Box 94, Gardner House, Hornbeam Park Avenue, Harrogate, N.Yorks. HG2 8XE
01423 844000

'The fund aims to invest in those companies which make a positive contribution to the environment. Some companies which have a "neutral" stance may not be making a positive contribution but are considered not to be making a negative or detrimental contribution to the environment, may be chosen to provide a balanced portfolio.

Our criteria are: animal testing, greenhouse gas emissions from fossil fumes [sic], road/air transport, companies conducting business with the military, nuclear power, ozone depleting chemicals, pesticides, pollution convictions, pornography, road building, South Africa, third world exploitation, tropical hardwood, water pollution and convictions, corporate giving, and charity giving'.

Jupiter Ecology Fund, and International Green Investment Fund

Jupiter Asset Management Ltd., Knightsbridge House, 197 Knightsbridge, London SW7 1RB
0171 412 0703

'Ethical Criteria:

• Alcoholic drinks: any company which derives in excess of 10 per cent of turnover from this industry will not be included on the Approved List.

• Armaments: Any company which derives in excess of 1 per cent of turnover from this industry will not be included on the Approved List.

• Gambling: Any company which derives in excess of 1 per cent of turnover from this industry will not be included on the Approved List.

• Nuclear power: Any company which derives in excess of 1 per cent of turnover from this industry will not be included on the Approved List.

• Pornographic publications: Any company which derives in excess of 1 per cent of turnover from this activity will not be included on the Approved List.

• Tobacco: Any company which derives in excess of 1 per cent of turnover from this industry will not be included on the Approved List.

Positive Criteria:

• Animal Testing: The Research Unit seeks to establish that companies are actively seeking to minimise their involvement in animal testing. This involves companies making a commitment to the "Three Rs": reduction, refinement and replacement of tests. The exception is in the case of cosmetic products: companies in this business which have failed to set a fixed cut-off date for the total cessation of their involvement with animal testing, or do not operate the 'five year rule' – which requires the avoidance of products tested on animals within five years – will be barred from the Approved List. In the case of companies which operate the five year rule, the Research Unit encourages the adoption of a fixed cut-off date.

• Uniform Global Operating Standards: The Research Unit considers global operating standards. This encompasses workers rights as well as environmental issues. This is a complex area, especially for companies that expand through acquisition, however the Research Unit looks for companies' commitment to converge standards in all operations to meet best practice.

• Equal Opportunities and Community Involvement: pro-active policies for enhancing employment opportunities – addressing issues such as the provision of training, childcare facilities, flexible working hours and wheelchair access. The Research Unit also requests companies to provide information on donations to, or sponsorship of, community projects, or support for social programmes. Other important indicators of corporate social responsibility include membership of organisations with a social remit such as Business in the Community's 'Per Cent Club'.

Environmental Criteria:

• Emissions and Effluents: emissions to air, water and land, including noise and other nuisances.

• Waste: the production of waste and the failure to recover, recycle and dispose of it safely.

• Energy Consumption: inefficient use of energy and the use of non-renewable fuels.

• Raw Materials: the unsustainable use of input materials.

• Transportation: the inefficient movement of goods.

• Land Use: the failure to protect places of amenity or wildlife value, and the use of green field in preference to brown field sites.

• Corporate Environmental Policy: whether the company publishes an environmental policy statement, what action the policy commits the company to take, how the policy is communicated to employees and whether it is publicly available.

• Environmental management: How structured is a company's approach to environmental management. An undertaking to apply the British Standard Institute's BS7750 on Environmental Management Systems or the European Community's Eco-Management and Audit Scheme is regarded as a good indicator of commitment.

• Monitoring Environmental Impact: How well a company monitors its own environmental performance. The principal tool for such monitoring is the environmental audit. To be most useful, audits should be regular and conducted, or verified by a third party.

• Disclosure: How well a company discloses information on environmental performance. The Research Unit places emphasis on the quantification of the information that is disclosed and the company's annual performance in relation to stated targets.

- Trading Partner Assessments: How rigorously a company assesses the environmental performance of its trading partners. This principally refers to suppliers but can also cover the performance of contractions. The Research Unit attaches great importance to the 'cradle to grave approach' to assessment and therefore favours companies that have considered the impact of all their operations, from raw material extraction through to final disposal. The Unit assesses the mechanisms – such as questionnaires, audits and dialogue – that companies use in their supply-chain scrutiny.
- Energy Efficiency: How effective a company is at reducing its energy consumption. The Research Unit enquires whether companies have recognised the principle of 'continuous improvement' by setting continuous improvement targets for energy efficiency.
- Responsibility: Whether environmental responsibility rests with a main board director and how much of that person's time is spent on environmental issues. The Research Unit also enquires whether there is a formal hierarchy of environmental accountability throughout the company.
- Environmental Communication: How fully employees are informed about, and involved in, environmental issues, and the extent of the provision of training relating to the environment.
- Legal Compliance: The Research Unit assess whether the company is, or has been, the subject of prosecution or litigation or has otherwise attracted adverse attention from regulatory bodies.
- Products and Services: The extent that products and services promote environmental improvement by reducing harmful emissions, waste or resource depletion; the commitment to the research and development of products which may assist environmental performance in the future; and whether packaging is minimised and if it is biodegradable or reclaimable, and the information given to the consumer about contents'.

Lincoln National Green Fund

Lincoln Investment Management Ltd., The Quays, 101-105 Oxford Road, Uxbridge, Middlesex UB8 1LZ
01895 200200

The fund invests directly into the Jupiter Ecology Fund (see above) and their criteria are therefore identical.

MI Ethical Fund

Merchant Investors Assurance, St Batholomew's House, Lewins Mead, Bristol BS1 2NH
0117 926 6366

'Eligible organisations must demonstrate a responsible attitude to the environment and community, both local and global, and practice good worker/management relations and fair treatment for their employees.

Organisations associated with armaments, nuclear processing, oppressive regimes, tobacco and alcohol production, experimentation on animals and environmental damage will be avoided'.

NPI Global Care Income Unit Trust, NPI Global Care Pension Fund, NPI Global Care Unit Trust, NPI Global Care Pension Managed Fund

National Provident Investment Managers Ltd., PO Box 227, 48 Gracechurch Street, London EC3P 3HH
0171 623 4200

NPI Global Care Unit Trust and *NPI Global Care Pension Fund:*
'The funds invest in companies with products and practices which enhance the quality of the environment and the life of the community. Investments will not be made in companies which adversely affect people, animals or the environment.

Areas the trust will support:

• Community involvement: companies active in the community with programmes which may include staff secondment, support of "Business in the Community", the "Per cent Club" or charitable giving and fund raising.

• Education and training: as needs in the workplace change, training is becoming increasingly important in providing new skills for young people or those who have been out of employment. We look for companies supplying education or training services to heighten the quality of life and opportunity in schools and the workplace.

• Healthcare services: we look for companies supplying medical equipment, specialist nursing services, care for the long-term disabled or elderly, or holistic therapies.

• Health and safety services: we look for companies supplying medical equipment, specialist nursing services, care for the long term disabled or elderly, or holistic therapies.

• Health and safety equipment: we look for companies supplying specialist equipment or devices which have health and safety applications.

• Good employee relations: we look for companies with good industrial relations records and policies including, for example, measures to encourage employee participation, support for women and minorities, and Employee Share Ownership Plans.

• Policy statements, audits and openness: companies with clear policies and systems of accountability. For example those which publish a statement of business ethics or code of conduct, have environment management systems (such as EMAS or BS7750) or conduct social audits and make them publicly available and respond fully to external inquiries.

• Progressive relations and strategy: companies which clearly explain their corporate strategy and its environmental and social implication. Companies which actively promote the interests of staff such as maternity/paternity leave, counselling services, pension schemes or other welfare services; customers, for example those with eco-labelling of products; suppliers such as those carrying out audits for environmental performance and fair trade; and the public, such as those which contribute to community activities.

- Effective corporate governance: companies which display accountability to their investors and seek to comply with the recommendations of the Cadbury Committee on corporate governance.

- Energy conservation: we look for companies engaged in the supply of energy conservation services such as domestic or industrial insulation, or electronic energy efficiency devices.

- Mass transit systems: we look for companies providing bus and rail services or which manufacture bicycles.

- Multimedia and telecommunications: we look for companies directly transforming the use of information, communication or ways of working, including developments in CD-ROMs, video conferencing, teleworking or mobile telephones.

- Pollution monitoring/pollution control equipment: we look for companies engaged in the manufacture, supply or operation of pollution control equipment or monitoring devices.

- Process control equipment: companies manufacturing or supplying efficiency improvement devices which provide water, energy or materials savings.

- Recycling services: we look for companies which collect and recycle waste or which use a high proportion of recycled waste in their products.

- Renewable energy: we look for companies involved in generating electricity from renewable resources such as wind, solar and hydro power.

- Water management: we look for companies involved in protecting and providing water supplies, or providing water purification services or equipment.

- Animals: we look for companies active in processing or selling vegetarian foods, and companies developing alternative textiles to leather.

Areas the trust will not support:

- Alcohol: we seek to avoid companies producing alcoholic drinks or which generate more than 10 per cent of their turnover from its sale.

- Gambling: we avoid companies with activities related to gambling, including the National Lottery and ownership and operation of betting shops, horse and greyhound racing tracks, licensed bingo halls, casinos and gaming clubs.

- Irresponsible marketing: we avoid companies which have consistently had public complaints upheld against them by the Advertising Standards Authority or have irresponsibly marketed products such as breast milk substitutes to developing countries.

- Armaments: we avoid companies selling or producing strategic goods or services for military weapons or operations.

- Oppressive regimes: we avoid companies with subsidiaries or associated interests which support the activities of oppressive regimes, or companies which use forced labour.

- Pornography: companies publishing, printing, or distributing newspapers or magazines, or distributing films and videos classed as pornographic are excluded from our portfolio.

- Tobacco: we avoid companies which engage in activities related to the production of tobacco products or generate more than 10 per cent of turnover from tobacco sales.
- Greenhouse gases: the trust will avoid energy companies generating high emissions of carbon dioxide, the main greenhouse gas. Also excluded are companies involved in the extraction, refining or distribution of fossil fuels (except natural gas); oil exploration and distribution; and fossil fuel power stations which use coal or oil.
- Mining: companies directly involved in mining or quarrying are avoided.
- Nuclear power: companies are avoided which are involved in the uranium fuel cycle, treat radioactive waste, or supply nuclear related equipment or services for constructing or running nuclear plant or facilities.
- The ozone layer: the trust will not invest in companies which make or sell ozone depleting chemicals or users of ozone depleting chemicals which have yet to set a date to phase them out.
- Pesticides: we will avoid companies which manufacture, store, wholesale or retail pesticide products in the UK which are on the Department of the Environment 'Red List', which have been restricted in five or more countries, or implicated in incidents investigated by the Health and Safety Executive.
- Road builders: we avoid companies generating more than 10 per cent of their turnover from roadbuilding.
- Tropical hardwood: companies active in the extraction, clearing, processing or imports of tropical hardwood are avoided.
- Water pollution: companies consistently exceeding discharge consents are not included in the portfolio.
- Animal testing: companies manufacturing pharmaceuticals, medicines, vitamins, cosmetics, soaps, or toiletries are not included unless they make it clear that their products or ingredients are not animal tested.
- Fur: companies involved in the sale or manufacture of animal fur products are excluded.
- Meat/dairy production: any companies involved in the production, processing of meat products, and meat/poultry related products including dairy products and eggs, or whose primary activity involves their sale are excluded from the portfolio'.

The NPI Global Care Income Unit Trust and *Global Care Pension Managed Fund*:

'The fund will invest in companies which demonstrate a positive contribution to social wellbeing and the protection and wise use of the natural environment. Investment will also be made in companies which the managers believe could, with encouragement, make a greater contribution to these objectives. The trust aims to encourage positive change across industry.

The trust supports businesses of direct social and environmental benefit. The managers talk to companies to encourage positive social and environmental change. The trust invests in social banks and, by doing so, supports smaller enterprises and projects which have a high beneficial impact for communities.

The trust will invest in companies with the positive attributes listed for the Global Care Unit Trust and Global Care Pension Fund [education and training, healthcare services, health and safety, employee relations, policy statements and audits, progressive community relationships, effective corporate governance, energy conservation, mass transit systems, multimedia and telecommunications, pollution monitoring and control, recycling services, renewable energy and water management.]

The funds avoids companies working in the following areas: armaments, nuclear industry, tobacco, animal testing, and contentious industries such as mining, oil, chemicals, and car manufacture or in companies using animal testing unless the company can demonstrate an outstandingly positive response towards environmental or social concerns'.

The Global Care Pension Managed Fund will invest 'in a well spread portfolio of assets. These include UK and overseas equities, property, fixed interest stocks or bonds which meet the social criteria'.

Scottish Equitable Ethical Unit Trust and Ethical Pension Fund

Scottish Equitable Fund Managers Ltd., 28 St Andrews Square, Edinburgh, EH2 1YF
0131 556 9101

'The following companies are not currently considered suitable for ethical investment:

• Any company which manufactures armaments or nuclear weapons.

• Any company involved in the production of nuclear fuels, or which supplies the nuclear power industry.

• Any company which donates more than £10,000pa to any political party or organisation.

• Any company which has had repeated public complaints upheld against it by the Advertising Standards Authority in the last two years.

• Any company whose investment in betting shops, casinos, amusement arcades, or the fruit machine industry accounts for more than 10 per cent of its total business.

• Any company for which the brewing, distillation or sale of alcoholic drinks accounts for more than 10 per cent of its total business.

• Any company which conducts any kind of experiments on animals or which manufactures or sells animal tested cosmetics or pharmaceuticals.

• Any company for which the growing, processing or sale of tobacco products accounts for more than 10 per cent of its total business.

• Any company which sells animal fur products.

• Any company which has any involvement in the production, processing or sale of meat and poultry products.

• As we are unable to obtain sufficient information on the companies, organisations, or institutions to which banks lend money, all banks are excluded'.

Skandia Ethical Selection Fund

Skandia Life, PO Box 37, Skandia House, Portland Terrace, Southampton SO9 7BX
01703 334411

'Screening is based on the following negative issues: armaments and nuclear weapons, animal exploitation and experimentation, oppressive regimes, alcohol, tobacco, environmentally damaging practices, gambling and pornography.

The following positive issues are considered: environmental protection, pollution control, conservation and recycling, safety and security, medicine and healthcare, equal opportunity provision for employees'.

Sovereign Ethical Fund

Sovereign Unit Trust Managers Ltd., Tringham House, Wessex Fields, Deansleigh Road, Bournemouth BH7 7DT
01202 435400

'• The fund managers will seek to invest in those companies whose products or business activities contribute to the improvement of the environment.

• Companies which display an awareness of environmental issues are likely to be selected as candidates for investment.

• Investments may be made in those companies that are actively taking steps to reduce their negative impact on the environment.

• The fund managers will seek to invest in those companies who are known to be good employers with a sound employment record including equal rights.

• Investments may be made in companies which contribute to society generally by supporting local community, national or worldwide projects.

• The fund does not invest in companies which derive more than 1 per cent of their pre-tax profits from any country with oppressive political, social or employment measures.

• The fund will aim to avoid companies that manufacture armaments or weapon systems as well as those involved in the construction of non-civilian military facilities.

• The fund will seek to avoid investing in companies which have any involvement in the production of alcohol or tobacco, or those which derive more than 10 per cent of their profits from the distribution or sale of these products. In addition it will not invest in any company which earns more than 10 per cent of its profits from gambling activities.

• Companies whose activities include nuclear processing or which derive a significant proportion of their profits from involvement with the nuclear industry are excluded.

• The fund will aim to avoid those companies which manufacture cosmetics which have been tested on animals; produce any items which contain ingredients obtained from endangered species or are involved in the manufacture of fur coats or similar articles'.

Sun Life Global Portfolio Ecological Fund

Sun Life Group, 107 Cheapside, London EC2V 6DU
0171 447 8080

This company was contacted a number of times requesting details of their fund, but no information was supplied.

TSB Environmental Investor Fund

TSB Unit Trusts Ltd., Charlton Place, Andover, Hants SP10 1RE
01264 346794

'Stocks are selected on the basis of investment merit, provided that they qualify under one of 11 environmental categories'. (The 11 categories are not specified).

The United Charities Ethical Trust

Family Assurance Friendly Society, 16-17 West Street, Brighton BN1 2RL
01273 725272

'The portfolio has been checked against the following criteria:

A. Alcohol. Company groups which derive more than 33% of their reported annual turnover from the production or sale of alcoholic drinks

B. Animal Tested Cosmetic Products. Company groups which manufacture cosmetics or toiletry products unless they confirm that they and their ingredients suppliers have not tested either the products or ingredients on animals since particular dates.

C. Animal Testing Services. Company groups which provide animal testing services.

D. Human Rights. Company groups which include a subsidary or associated company registered in at least five of the countries with [sic] Freedom House has given a rating of 6.5 or worse.

E. Intensive Farming Methods. Company groups which derive any turnover from poultry farming or pig farming unless intensive methods are not used.

F. Intensive Farming – Fish Farming. Company groups which own or operate a fish farm.

G. Intensive Farming – Abattoir. Company groups which own or operate at least one abattoir or poultry slaughterhouse or poultry processing plant.

H. Military – Weapons. Company groups which have been involved in the sale or production of weapons systems.

I. Military – Nuclear Weapons. Company groups which have been involved in the sale or product [sic] of nuclear weapons systems.

J. Military – Any Exports. Company groups which have been involved in the export of goods or services for military use or which have exhibited at defence equipment exhibitions.

K. Mining / Quarrying. Company groups which derive any turnover from mining or quarrying.

L. Nuclear Power – Nuclear Only. Company groups which have derived any turnover from the uranium fuel cycle, handle radioactive waste, or supply nuclear-related equipment or services for nuclear plant or facilities.

M. Ozone Depleting Chemicals – Any Chemical Supply. Company groups which supply ozone depleting chemicals (ODCs).

N. Pesticides – Red List. Company groups which have received approval from MAFF or HSE to market pesticide products in the UK which include active ingredients on the Red List.

O. Pesticides – Banned. Company groups which have received approval from MAFF or HSE to market pesticide products in the UK which include active ingredients that are banned or restricted in five or more countries.

P. Pollution Convictions. Company groups which have been convicted during the period covered following a prosecution by Her Majesty's Inspectorate of Pollution in England and Wales or Her Majesty's Industrial Pollution Inspectorate in Scotland.

Q. Third World – Tobacco Market. Company groups which market tobacco products in the Third World.

R. Tobacco. Company groups which derive more than 10% of their reported annual turnover from the production or sale of tobacco or tobacco products.

S. Tobacco Production – Any. Company groups which derive any turnover from the production of tobacco or tobacco products.

T. Tropical Hardwood Retail. Company groups which EIRIS has estimated retail more than 2000 cubic metres of tropical hardwood joinery, timber or furniture annually, excluding any from sustainable sources.

U. Tropical Hardwood Use. Company groups which EIRIS has estimated use more than 2000 cubic metres of tropical hardwood in construction, joinery or furniture manufacture annually excluding any from sustainable sources.

V. Tropical Hardwood – Import/Merchant. Company groups which import, process or merchant timber, unless tropical-hardwood-free or from sustainable forests.

W. Tropical Hardwood – Mining etc. Company groups which engage in mining or other activity in tropical regions unless tropical forests are not cleared.

X. Tropical Hardwood – Extract. Company groups which extract tropical timber excluding any from sustainable forests.

Y. Water – Any. Company groups which have exceeded at least one parameter on a discharge consent in the full period covered.

Z. Water. Company groups which have exceeded their discharge consents in the last year covered more than 35 times.

a. Water Convicts. Company groups which have been convicted during the period covered following a prosecution by the NRA or by an RPB and fined more than £4000.00 on at least one occasion.

The fund covenants part of its profits to Action for Blind People, the Country Landowners Association Charitable Trust, Guide Dogs for the Blind, Mencap City Foundation, and the Royal Society for the Protection of Birds'.

Appendix 3

Institutions offering tailor-made ethical investments

These institutions will compile investment portfolios with ethical or Green criteria for wealthy investors. They normally set a minimum sum they will invest on this basis.

Albert E. Sharp Ethical PEP
2 Trinity Street, College Green, Bristol BS1 5TE
0117 926 0051
The minimum sum they will invest for an individual is £50,000.

Cantrade Investment Management Ltd.
4 Chiswell Street, London EC1Y 4UP
0171 614 8000
The minimum sum they will invest for an individual is £500,000.

Duncan Lawrie Ltd.
1 Hobart Place, London SW1W 0HU
0171 245 1234
The minimum sum they will invest for an individual is £100,000.

Friends Provident Life Office
15 Old Bailey, London EC4M 7AP
0171 329 4454
The minimum sum they will invest for an individual is £40,000 though they also run unit trusts – see Appendix 2.

Grant Thornton Personal Financial Planning Ltd.
Elgin House, Billing Road, Northampton NN1 5AU
01604 27811
No minimum set.

Granville Investment Management Ltd.
Mint House, 77 Mansell Street, London E1 8AF
0171 418 1212
The minimum sum invested for individuals is £75,000.

Henderson Financial Management

3 Finsbury Avenue, London EC2M 2PA

0171 638 5757

The minimum sum invested for an individual is £150,000 but they also run a unit trust – see Appendix 2.

Henry Cooke Lumsden

1 King Street, Manchester M2 6AW

0161 834 2332

The minimum sum invested for individuals is £40,000.

Mercury Asset Management PLC.

33 King William Street, London EC4R 9AS

0171 280 2800

The minimum sum they will invest for individuals is £10,000.

Appendix 4

Insurance companies

Companies offering building, contents, or vehicle insurance policies with an environmental connection:

Ethical Investors Group
See Appendix 1

Naturesave Policies Ltd.
42 Henley Street, Oxford OX4 1ES
01865 242280

Companies that may be considered ethical on different grounds:

Co-operative Insurance Society Ltd
Miller Street, Manchester M60 0AL
0161 832 8686

Ecclesiastical Insurance Group plc
Beaufort House, Brunswick Road, Gloucester GL1 1JZ
01452 528533

Appendix 5

Funds, companies, banks, building societies and organisations in the social economy accepting investments

Archway Resource Centre, 1a Waterlow Road, Archway, London N19 5NJ. 0171 281 0919

Aston Reinvestment Trust (ART), Swan House, Hospital Street & Summer Lane, Birmingham B19 3PY. 0121 236 4808

The Barnet Green Co-op Ltd., 13 Sunny Gardens Road, Hendon, London NW4 1SL. 0181 203 2834

The Bioregional Charcoal Company Ltd., Sutton Ecology Centre, Honeywood Walk, Carshalton, Surrey SM5 3NX. 0181 669 0713

The CAF Social Investment Fund, Charities Aid Foundation, 25 Kings Hill Avenue, Kings Hill, West Malling, Kent ME19 4TA. 01732 520 000

The Catholic Building Society, 7 Strutton Ground, London SW1P 2HY. 0171 222 6736

Centre for Alternative Technology PLC, Machynlleth, Powys, Wales SY20 9AZ. 01654 702400

The Co-operative Bank PLC, PO Box 101, 1 Balloon Street, Manchester M60 4EP. 0161 832 3456

Co-operative Retail Services, 29 Dantzic Street, Manchester M4 4BA. 0161 832 8152

Cornerstone Housing Co-operative, 16 Sholebrooke Avenue, Leeds LS7 3HB. 0113 262 9365

Ecogroco Housing Co-operative Ltd., PO Box 5, Lostwithiel, Cornwall PL22 OYT. 01726 850500

The Ecology Building Society, 18 Station Road, Cross Hills, nr Keighley, West Yorks. BD20 7EH. 0345 697758

The Ecological Trading Co PLC, 659 Newark Road, Lincoln LN6 8SA. 01522 501850

Industrial Common Ownership Finance Ltd., 12-14 Gold Street, Northampton NN1 1RS. 01604 37563

The Local Investment Fund, Business in the Community, 8 Stratton Street, London W1X 6AH. 0171 629 1600

Out of This World, 52 Elswick Road, Newcastle Upon Tyne NE4 6JH. 0191 272 1601

Paperback Ltd., Unit 2, Bow Triangle Business Centre, Eleanor Street, London E3 4NP. O181 980 2233

Phoenix (MK) Housing Co-operative, Phoenix House, 205 Beadlemead, Netherfield, Milton Keynes MK6 4HU. 01908 606409

Radical Routes Ltd., 24 South Road, Hockley, Birmingham B18 5NB. 0121 551 1132

Red Pepper, 3 Gunthorpe Street, London E1 7RP. 0171 247 1702

Scottish Community Enterprise Investment Fund PLC, Unit 45, Society Place, West Calder, West Lothian EH55 8EA. 01506 871370

Shared Interest, 31 Moseley Street, Newcastle-Upon-Tyne NE1 1HX. 0191 261 5943

Shared Visions, 8 Helen Road, Oxford OX2 ODE. 01865 721922

Swanage Family Housing Association, 4 Streche Road, Swanage, Dorset BH19 1NF. 01929 425627

Tools for Self Reliance Cymru, Pen Isaf Pentre, Tretower, Crickhowell, Powys, Wales NP8 1RD. 01874 730155

Totnes Investment in Local Trade (TILT), The Community Office, Birdwood House, 44 High Street, Totnes, Devon TQ9 4SG. 01803 867099

Traidcraft PLC, Kingsway, Gateshead NE11 ONE. 0191 491 0591

Triodos Bank, Brunel House, 11 The Promenade, Clifton, Bristol BS8 3NN. 0117 973 9339

The Wind Company Ltd., Unit 29, Trinity Enterprise Centre, Furness Business Park, Barrow in Furness, Cumbria LA14 2PN. 01229 821028

The Wind Fund PLC, Brunel House, 11 The Promenade, Clifton, Bristol BS8 3NN. 0117 973 9339

Appendix 6

Organisations with an interest in ethical investment

ARIES – Social Economy On Line, 51 Rue de la Concorde, B-1050 Brussels, Belgium. Tel. + 32 2 513 75 01. Internet: aries.brussels@geo2.poptel. org.uk Geonet: GEO2:ARIES-BRUSSELS

ARIES provides on-line information on a wide range of topics concerning the social economy including details of funding opportunities, tenders, media reviews, seminars and conferences.

Association of British Credit Unions Ltd., Unit 307, Westminster Business Square, 339 Kennington Lane, London SE11 5QY. 0171 582 2626

ABCUL promotes the formation and growth of credit unions by providing training and education and acting as a voice for the movement.

Christian Ethical Investment Group (CEIG), Secretary: Canon Bill Whiffen, 90 Booker Avenue, Bradwell Common, Milton Keynes, MK13 8EF. 01908 677 466

CEIG exists to promote a stronger ethical investment policy in the Church of England. It holds meetings during the Church's General Synod and runs regular seminars.

Delphi International Ltd., 36 Great Queen Street, London WC2B 5AA. 0171 404 2963

Delphi is a financial advisory firm which helps institutions and fund managers benefit from the investment opportunities arising out of the worldwide shift to more environmentally-sustainable development. It does not normally work with individual members of the public.

Ethical Investment Research Services (EIRIS), 504 Bondway Business Centre, 71 Bondway, London SW8 1SQ. 0171 735 1351

EIRIS produce regular lists of ethical and green financial advisers and unit trusts and publish a newsletter. They also screen stock market companies in the UK and the rest of Europe for a wide range of positive and negative criteria.

International Association of Investors in the Social Economy (INAISE), Rue d'Arlon 40, B-1040 Brussels, Belgium. + 32 2 230 30 57

INAISE exists to promote and support financial organisations which invest in enterprises of an ethical, ecological, cultural and self-managing nature including projects run by women, ethnic minorities, people with disabilities and in the Third World.

New Consumer, 52 Elswick Road, Newcastle Upon Tyne NE4 6JH. 0191 272 1148
New Consumer is a research organisation which produces reports on the social and
ethical policies of companies. They also campaign for companies to adopt best practice in their areas. Their reports include a number which compare the ethical
performance of particular companies.

New Economics Foundation, Vine Court, 112-116 Whitechapel Road, London E1
 1JE. 0171 377 5696
NEF exists as a think tank to promote new economics to both ordinary people and
economists. It undertakes research into all aspects of the social economy and ethical
and green investment.

Pensions Investment Research Centre Ltd. (PIRC), 147-157 St John Street,
 London EC1V 4QJ. 0171 250 3311
PIRC is a research and investment advisor acting on behalf of financial institutions
such as pension funds, investment managers etc. which use ethical and green criteria
in their investment decisions. They campaign for institutions to exercise their power
as active shareholders by proposing and voting on resolutions.

Personal Investment Authority, 1 Canada Square, Canary Wharf, London E14
 5AZ. 0171 538 8860
The PIA is the body responsible for regulating financial advisers who work with
individual members of the public.

Social Investment Forum, c/o New Economics Foundation, Vine Court, 112-116
 Whitechapel Road, London E1 1JE. 0171 377 5907
The Forum's primary purpose is to promote and encourage the development and
positive impact of Socially Responsible Investment throughout the UK. They run
regular seminars with business leaders and politicians, and publish a newsletter.

Other organisations concerned with ethical issues or investment

Baby Milk Action, 23 St Andrews St., Cambridge CB2 1AA. 01223 464420
Building Societies Members Association, 6 Bramley Court, Marden, Kent TN12
 9QN. 01622 831904
Campaign Against The Arms Trade, 11 Goodwin Street, Finsbury Park, London
 N4 3HQ. 0171 281 0297
Centre for the Study of Financial Innovation, 18 Curzon Street, London W1Y
 7AD. 0171 493 0173
Fairtrade Association, 105 Euston St., London NW1 2ED. 0171 383 0425
Friends of the Earth, 26-28 Underwood Street, London N1 7JQ. 0171 490 1555
Green Party, 1a Waterlow Road, London N19 5NJ. 0171 272 4474
Greenpeace, Canonbury Villas, Highbury London N1 2PN. 0171 354 5100
LetsLink UK, 61 Woodcock Road, Warminster, Wilts. BA12 9DH. 01985 217871

Lets Solutions, 68 Ashford Road, Withington, Manchester M20 9EH. 0161 434 8712

National Association of Bank Customers, Llanthony Secunda Manor, Church Road, Caldicot, Gwent NP6 4HT. 01291 430009

National Federation of Progressive Co-operators, 113 Park Road, Loughborough LE11 2HD

Private Equity Funding Association, PO Box 127, Hereford HR4 OYN. 01432 342484

ProShare Investment Clubs, Library Chambers, 13-14 Basinghall Street, London EC2V 5BQ. 0171 600 0984

Safe Alliance (Sustainable Agriculture, Food and Environment Alliance), 38 Edbury Street, London SW1W OLU

Soil Association, 86 Colston Street, Bristol BS1 5BB. 0117 929 0661

Struggle Against Financial Exploitation (SAFE), 5 Great Chapel Street, London W1V 3AG. 0171 437 1123

The UK Shareholders Association, Half Tiles, Roseacre Gardens, Chilworth, Surrey GU4 8RQ. 01483 561228

World Development Movement, 25 Beehive Place, London SW9 7QR. 0171 737 6215

Appendix 7

Periodicals

Christian Ethical Investment Group Newsletter. Editor: John Fleetwood, 12 Coquet Terrace, Heaton, Newcastle-upon-Tyne NE6 5LD. 0191 265 9836

Gives information on how the Christian community are adopting ethical criteria when investing.

The ENDS Report, Environmental Data Services Ltd., Unit 24, 40 Bowling Green Lane, London EC1R ONE. 0171 278 4745

The ENDS Report provides detailed information on the environmental record of companies, news of corporate governance issues, and changes in environmental law affecting business.

The Ethical Consumer, 16 Nicholas Street, Manchester M1 4EJ 0161 237 1630

The EC is primarily aimed at consumers, but includes a regular section on ethical finance and banking. It regularly assesses companies for their environmental and social performance and includes a page of 'boycott news' listing firms which organisations have asked consumers to boycott.

The Ethical Investor, published by EIRIS (see Appendix 6).

A newsletter covering all aspects of ethical investment with details of new funds launched, interviews with people in the industry and corporate governance issues.

Greenpeace Business, Greenpeace, Canonbury Villas, London N1 2PN. 0171 354 5100

Greenpeace Business gives an overview of how businesses in the UK and abroad are responding to environmental pressures.

ICOF Newsletter, published by Industrial Common Ownership Finance Ltd. (see Appendix 5).

Newsletter focusing mainly on the work of worker co-operatives and other sectors of the social economy.

Labour Research, magazine of the Labour Research Department, 78 Blackfriars Road, London SE1 8HF. 0171 928 3649

Newsletter giving details of the Department's researches on company giving to political parties, wage rates, working conditions etc.

New Economics, newsletter of the New Economics Foundation (see Appendix 6).

It reports on new initiatives and research in all aspects of the economy, including green and ethical investment and the social economy.

New Money, 92 Folly Lane, St Albans, Herts AL3 5JH. 01727 837462

New Money is a 'financial newsletter for people interested in new ideas' and describes itself as 'a bit alternative'. Its articles span the entire ethical investment world and also stray into subjects such as Zen pension plans and the Tao of pension planning. It is published by financial adviser Robin Currie who is a representative of the Manulife Group.

New Sector, Society Place, West Calder EH55 8EA. 01506 871370

New Sector is the magazine of community and co-operative enterprises and sets out to promote new economic values, economic activity which centres on people and new concepts of economic development and growth. It covers the activities of workers' co-operatives and community owned businesses.

The Social Investment Forum, newsletter of the Forum (see Appendix 6).

Examines all developments in the world of the social economy, including banking, large and small companies, and shareholder rights.

Appendix 8

Further reading

Bankwatch, edited by Ed Mayo, published by the New Economics Foundation (see Appendix 6).

Bankwatch is a study of the credentials, accountability and ethics of the banks, drawn from a new economics perspective.

Environmental and Financial Performance: Are They Related? Mark Cohen, Scott Fenn and Jonathan Naimon, The Investor Responsibility Research Centre, 1350 Connecticut Avenue, NW Suite 700, Washington DC, 20036-1701 USA.

A study of the relationship between environmental and financial performance of US quoted companies.

The Ethical Investor, Russell Sparkes, HarperCollins. ISBN 000 627863 9

'Illustrates how ethical investment empowers people in a practical way. They may choose to benefit the causes important to them, including women's rights, rain forests, the status of workers in the Third World, or alternative technologies. They may equally choose not to support businesses which case only for profit and not for the harmful consequences of their exploits. The book shows how ethical investors forced change on South Africa and how they are currently fighting for the environment'.

Green Funds: An Instrument of Change, Nicholas Schoenberger, Wye College, University of London

An unpublished MSc study of green and ethical funds, shareholder power, and corporate responsibility.

An Independent Guide to Ethical and Green Investment Funds, published by Holden Meehan (see Appendix 1).

An annual list of ethical and green funds assessed by a number of criteria, and with details of whether they offer unit trusts, pensions, PEPs and life assurance. The guide also takes investors through some of the issues to consider before investing.

Invested in the Common Good, Susan Meeker-Lowry, New Society Publishers (distributed in the UK by Jon Carpenter Publishing, The Spendlove Centre, Charlbury OX7 3PQ). ISBN 0-86571-292-1

A US book describing how to invest in community banks and funds, operate shareholder boycotts, and operate organisations such as land banks, bartering and work exchange networks and community supported agriculture systems.

Investing for Good, Peter Kinder, Steven Lydenberg, Amy Domini. HarperBusiness. ISBN 0-88730-662-4

Written in the US by the principals of a major consultancy providing social research on US corporations. Takes the reader through all the steps involved in investing in American corporations.

Money & Ethics – a guide to pensions, PEPs, endowment mortgages and other ethical investment plans. EIRIS (for address, see Appendix 6).

This handbook guides investors through the funds investing in the Stock Exchange with details of policies, ways to invest, research methods, the presence of an independent committee, newsletters issued and methods of communicating with companies. Also included are summaries of how much involvement the funds have in the ethical issues surveyed by EIRIS.

Money Matters – taking charge of our money, our values and our lives. New Economics Foundation (for address, see Appendix 6).

Money Matters is a resource list and bibliography covering items and organisations involved in ethical investment, charitable giving, alternative approaches to money, and 'feeling comfortable with money'.

The Shareholder Action Handbook – Using shares to make companies more accountable. Craig Mackenzie, New Consumer. ISBN 1 897806 00 0

Explains what a company is, the relationship between shareholders and the directors, the scope for constructive dialogue, pressure and direct action; the strategies that individuals and groups can use to influence companies, and provides details of the legal background.

What has Ethical Investment to do with Ethics? Digby Anderson and others, The Social Affairs Unit. ISBN 0 907631 65 7

This pamphlet questions whether ethical investment is truly ethical as the funds use what the author term a 'bizarre' list of 'fashionable causes' which excludes such issues as 'adultery, deception, sponging off others, and sinking into sloth and moroseness in front of a television'.

Appendix 9

Glossary

Literature which claims to explain the wide range of financial services available has a jargon all of its own. An understanding of the meaning of many of these words will – unfortunately – be needed when looking at literature produced by most sectors of the financial services industry.

ANNUAL GENERAL MEETING The meeting of shareholders and directors which companies are obliged by law to hold. The meeting formally accepts the accounts, agrees the DIVIDEND and appoints directors and auditors.

ANNUITY The payment by an investor of a lump sum to an institution in return for a regular monthly payment back until death. Generally annuities are bought with the proceeds of pension plans when a person retires, and the amount paid each month will be dependent on your age and state of health.

ARTICLES OF ASSOCIATION Along with the MEMORANDUM OF ASSOCIATION, these are the contracts which set up a company and govern what it is legally allowed to do.

BARGAIN A transaction on the Stock Exchange – it may or may not be a bargain in the more usual sense of the word.

BEARS Investors who believe that prices of stocks and shares will fall.

BID The price at which a unit trust or other institution will buy units or shares from customers. The bid price will be lower than the OFFER price, the difference (known as the BID/OFFER SPREAD) being the institution's running cost and profit.

BID/OFFER SPREAD see BID.

BLUE CHIP The biggest and most profitable companies listed on the Stock Exchange. Generally the blue chip companies are seen as Britain's best, but only a few of them would probably warrant inclusion in a green or ethical investor's portfolio.

BOND A financial instrument whereby an investor loans money to a company, institution or government. The bond will state when and if the sum loaned will be repayable, and the rate of interest payable. Bonds can be bought from and sold to other investors, usually via a stockbroker.

BUILDING SOCIETIES Institutions which accept deposits which pay interest, the sums being mainly loaned to individuals to buy their homes. The societies are non-profit making institutions.

BULLS Investors who believe the prices of stocks and shares will rise.

CHURNING The practice of buying and selling stocks and shares, or recommending changing pensions, units trusts etc. purely so the broker can make the commission on the sale.

CLEARING BANKS Banks which are part of the clearing system which allows them to pay cheques, direct debits etc.

COMMITTEE OF REFERENCE Group of usually well-known people appointed by ethical and green funds to set the criteria to be adopted, and in some cases to draw up a list of companies suitable for inclusion in the investment portfolio.

COMPANIES LIMITED BY GUARANTEE The legal status used by companies which want LIMITED LIABILITY but do not wish to distribute their profits amongst shareholders. The liability of shareholders is normally limited to a nominal £1 shareholding should the company go into liquidation. Companies limited by guarantee generally operate in the SOCIAL ECONOMY.

CO-OPERATIVE An organisation set up as a business or to provide housing without making a profit for shareholders, and with the participants (tenants, workers or consumers) having equal rights of control. Co-operatives are generally registered with the Registrar of Friendly Societies who is the government official responsible for regulating such societies under the Industrial and Provident Society Act. See INDUSTRIAL & PROVIDENT SOCIETY.

COUPON The interest paid on a bond.

DEBENTURE A bond issued by a UK company which is secured on fixed assets.

DIVIDEND The sums paid out to shareholders when a company makes a profit. The dividend is usually paid every six months and is expressed as a proportion of each share held. The total of dividend paid out is not usually the total of the profits made: companies will usually retain some proportion of the profits to expand the business or keep in reserve.

ENTERPRISE INVESTMENT SCHEME Government scheme to encourage people to invest in newly-formed companies. Investors receive tax relief on their shareholdings.

ENVIRONMENT FUND A unit trust fund which invests in companies in the environment industry such as waste disposal, recycling, alternative energy etc.

ETHICAL INVESTMENT Placing money with a company or institution which meets certain ethical standards, rather than only targets of financial risk, profit and accessibility.

EQUITY The capital of a company, usually the ordinary shares.

FAIR TRADE ORGANISATION A company, usually involved in trading with Third World countries, which has a central philosophy of paying a fair sum for products or commodities.

FINANCIAL SERVICES ACT The Act which requires those providing financial advice or investment schemes to be qualified and registered.

FLOTATION The first issuing of shares by a company.

FRONT END LOADING The charging arrangement whereby the bulk of commissions on long term schemes such as life assurance and pensions are paid in the first few years. Thus if investors wish to back out of such schemes early, they will receive back less – possibly far less – than they paid in.

FT-SE or Footsie (the Financial Times-Stock Exchange 100-Share Index) The daily average of the share prices of the 100 largest companies on the UK Stock Exchange. The index is compiled from the sales of shares which are automatically notified to the Stock Exchange Council. It is presumed that if more people want to sell their shares than buy them and the FT-SE goes down, the economy is suffering, and vice versa. The FT Index includes the shares of 30 large companies, the FT-SE Mid 250 Index covers the 250 companies next in size after those on the FT-SE, and the FT-SE Actuaries 350 covers the next 350 companies.

GILTS or GILT EDGED SECURITIES BONDS issued by the UK government.

GREEN INVESTMENT Investing money in companies or organisations which meet certain green or environmental standards. Some green investors will include ethical issues in their philosophy.

GROSS YIELD TO REDEMPTION The total return an investor will receive on a BOND including interest payments and capital growth, expressed as a percentage of the bond's price.

INDUSTRIAL AND PROVIDENT SOCIETY A CO-OPERATIVE which is registered to accept LOAN STOCK from the public.

INTEREST The payment for the use of money.

INVESTMENT TRUST A company which invests in other companies' shares. The trust is normally listed on the Stock Exchange and its shares rise and fall according to the performance of the companies whose shares it owns.

LIFE ASSURANCE A savings scheme where investors pay in a set amount each month for a fixed period of time. The money is invested in stocks and shares. At the end of the period the accrued sum is paid back. If the investor dies at any time during the period the sum deemed to have accrued at the end is paid to dependents.

LIFE COMPANIES Institutions which sell life assurance and insurance policies. They are some of the institutions which now own some 60% of UK industry.

LIFE INSURANCE A savings scheme whereby an individual pays a set monthly sum which is invested and guarantees a lump sum to dependents should the investor die in specified circumstances. See LIFE ASSURANCE.

LIMITED LIABILITY The legal status which allows the owners or shareholders to be only liable for company debts up to the value of their individual shareholdings. Where a business does not have limited liability, the personal wealth of the owners could be seized by creditors if it went into liquidation. In return for limited liability protection, companies are obliged to file their accounts for public inspection, they must hold annual meetings of shareholders, and have to declare their legal status using the suffix Ltd or PLC in their company names.

LIQUIDATION The process whereby a company ceases to exist as a legal entity. Liquidation can be initiated by the directors or creditors.

LIQUIDITY The ease with which an investment can be turned to cash. Thus a pension plan is not very liquid as it will only pay out on a future date except with expensive penalties, while a building society deposit which can be withdrawn on demand is highly liquid.

LISTED COMPANY A company whose shares are listed for sale on the Stock Exchange.

LOAN The lending of money for a period, normally in return for interest.

LOAN STOCK A loan which pays a fixed rate of interest and is not covered by any SECURITY. The loan is normally given by an individual to a company or other organisation.

MATCHED BARGAIN MARKET The list of prospective buyers and sellers of shares maintained by a company not quoted on the Stock Exchange. The market is the only way a holder of shares can sell them, and the share price does not usually fluctuate.

MATURITY The date when a loan or bond will be repaid.

MEMORANDUM OF ASSOCIATION See ARTICLES OF ASSOCIATION

NEW ISSUE The creation and first sale of a company's shares. A new issue is normally the only time that an investor buying shares will pass their money to the company itself, rather than another investor.

OFFER The price at which an institution will sell shares or units to the public – see BID.

ORDINARY SHARE The shares in a company which allow the holder to receive a dividend based on profits, or risk a loss. Normally ordinary shares allow the holder to attend AGMs, put resolutions, and vote on matters such as the dividend and appointment of directors.

PENSION A method of saving whereby the investor agrees to pay in a fixed amount each month which is then invested in stocks and shares. When the investor retires, the accrued investments are sold, and the sum realised is used to buy an ANNUITY which pays the pension. See WITH PROFITS and INDEX-LINKED.

PENSION FUNDS The institutions which run pension schemes. Along with insurance companies, the pensions institutions own over 60% of UK stocks and shares. The funds are mutual societies, that is, any profits go to the pension holders rather than outside shareholders.

PEPs (Personal Equity Plans) A scheme introduced by the government to encourage individuals to invest in Stock Exchange companies. Up to certain limits, the income from investments in PEPs can be free of tax.

P/E RATIO (Price Earnings Ratio) The relationship between a company's share price and its profits. Used by investors to decide whether the price of a share matches expected dividends.

PERSONAL INVESTMENT AUTHORITY (PIA) The self regulating company set up to register financial advisers under the FINANCIAL SERVICES ACT. Working as an adviser without PIA authorisation is a criminal offence.

PREFERENCE SHARES Shares which give holders first option on DIVIDENDS. Normally the dividend paid is lower than that paid on ordinary shares.

PREMIUM The payment for unit trusts, pensions etc. Payments can be one-off, or at regular intervals.

PRIVATE COMPANY A company whose shares are not on sale to the general public and whose shareholders carry LIMITED LIABILITY for any debts if the company goes into liquidation. They must include the suffix Ltd in the title name, and cannot be listed on the Stock Exchange. See PUBLIC COMPANY.

PUBLIC COMPANY A company whose shares can be bought by the general public. The name of public companies must include the suffix PLC, and only such companies can be LISTED on the Stock Exchange. Like PRIVATE COMPANIES the shareholders carry LIMITED LIABILITY for any debts if the company goes into LIQUIDATION.

QUOTED COMPANY A company listed on the Stock Exchange whose shares are available for anyone to buy.

REAL INTEREST RATE The profit to be made on an investment after inflation is excluded.

REDEMPTION DATE The date at which a BOND is repaid by the issuer.

RETAINED EARNINGS The profit which a company keeps rather than paying it to shareholders in the form of DIVIDENDS.

RIGHTS ISSUE The issuing of additional shares by a company.

SCREENING The practice of not investing in companies which fail to meet an investor's ethical standards.

SCRIP ISSUE The issuing of shares to existing shareholders. Sometimes scrip shares are issued because a company is revaluing its shares and therefore issuing a greater number, sometimes scrips are issued in lieu of cash dividends because they carry tax advantages.

SECONDARY MARKET A market whereby stocks and shares can be resold and where the price fluctuates day be day. A secondary market such as the Stock Exchange encourages investors to buy the shares of companies because they know it will be easy to sell them on if they need the cash. Secondary markets are the principal way of making money out of money rather than using it to facilitate the exchange of real goods and services.

SECURITIES Any financial asset which can be traded, such as STOCKS and SHARES and BONDS, but not bank or building society accounts.

SECURITY An asset pledged by a business or individual which can be claimed by a lender if the borrower defaults on a loan.

SHARES The ownership of a proportion of a company. See ORDINARY SHARES.

SOCIAL BANK A bank whose main aim is to provide loans to projects and businesses with social or environmental worth.

SOCIAL ECONOMY A generic term for companies, housing associations and co-operatives, fair trade charities and social banks whose primary aim is to provide the service they have been set up for in a fair and just way, and whose secondary aim is to return a profit or break even. In the conventional economy these priorities are generally reversed and making a profit is the primary aim. See COMPANIES LIMITED BY GUARANTEE.

SOCIALLY DIRECTED INVESTMENT (SDI) The practice of ensuring that money is invested in businesses or organisations which are contributing real worth to society. Distinguished from other forms of ethical investment which sometimes go no further than excluding companies doing harm.

SPREAD The difference between the price a financial institution will buy (the BID) and sell (the OFFER) securities. Investors will need to hold the security long enough before selling to cover the spread which constitutes the institution's profits.

STAMP DUTY The tax payable on a share transaction, generally a percentage of the price. The tax can be avoided if shares are transferred without payment.

STOCKBROKER An individual or firm licensed to buy and sell shares on other people's behalf.

STOCK EXCHANGE The market where shares and government bonds are bought and sold.

SUSTAINABILITY The ability of a company or organisation to operate without depleting the earth's resources or emitting pollution. A sustainable company does not use finite resources such as oil, gas or minerals, and does not emit pollutants such as greenhouse gases, ozone depleting chemicals, or those that damage water or soil.

TAX EXEMPT SPECIAL SAVINGS ACCOUNT (TESSA) A government plan allowing individuals to invest certain sums of money in bank and building society accounts and receive interest free of tax.

UNDERWRITE The agreement by financial institutions to buy any otherwise unsold stocks or shares when first issued. The institution is paid a fee in return for the undertaking, and the issuing company knows all its shares will be sold.

UNIT TRUST An institution which accepts money from individual investors and uses it to buy a spread of shares in different companies, thus reducing the risk for the investor. The institution will sell units to investors for more than they will buy them back – the SPREAD – and units cannot be sold onto other investors, they have to be returned to the issuing institution.

UNIVERSE The range of companies a fund or investor will select from. Thus a fund without any ethical criteria will have a large universe to choose from, while a fund with a tightly-drawn set of criteria will have a small universe.

VENTURE CAPITAL The money provided to a new company, usually by an institution or private investor. Such investments are seen as carrying high risk as the company management often have no previous record and there are inadequate assets to provide security. The money can be provided as a loan or in the form of shares, and if the company is successful a lot of money can be made – and vice versa.

YIELD The profit on a security.

Index

• •

Please note that the Appendices are not indexed

Low Impact Development

Planning and people in a sustainable countryside
Simon Fairlie

This complete re-examination of Britain's planning system from the bottom up – from the point of view of the planned, rather than of the planner – is an important contribution to the topical debate about the future and use of the countryside and what it means to achieve sustainability in the modern world.

Simon Fairlie argues that instead of excluding low income people from living and working in rural areas, planners should look favourably on proposals for low impact, environmentally benign homes and workplaces in the open countryside. Criteria for planning approval at present favour the wealthy commuter and the large-scale farmer and discriminate heavily against (e.g.) smallholders, low-impact homes, and experimental forms of husbandry.

The book is the result of much detailed research. It includes a number of cases studies of low impact developments, some of which received permission, some of which failed. It includes illustrations; policy recommendations; guides to acts of parliament, government circulars and policy guidelines etc.; references; and explanatory appendices. It is an invaluable tool both for those who wish to live on the land in a sustainable manner, and for planners and politicians who would like to make it possible for them to do so. As well as proposing changes to planning law, the author shows how existing regulations can be used to enable many environmentally benign projects to take place.

Simon Fairlie is an editor of *The Ecologist*, and co-author of *Whose Common Future?* (Earthscan, 1993). He writes for *The Guardian, New Statesman and Society*, and *Perspectives*.

£10 paperback 1 897766 25 4 176pp illustrated

Animal Rights

Extending the circle of compassion
Mark Gold

Essential reading for all those concerned about the treatment of animals. It discusses the extremely topical issues of cruel farming practices, live animal transportation, and the increasing trend towards meat-free diets.

• the most up-to-date and authoritative exposition of animal rights and the vegetarian and vegan case.

• provocatively links cruelty towards animals with a failure by humans to respect their own kind, demolishing the myth that animal rights campaigners care more about animals than about humans. Mark Gold shows how concern for animal welfare and animal rights has sprung from concern for human welfare and human rights, and gives examples to show how champions of the one have always been champions of the other too.

• an indictment of the violent and neo-fascist minorities who have tried to hi-jack the cause

• a telling analysis of the achievements of the last twenty years and a thought-provoking insight into both the problems and possibilities for future progress.

• persuasive evidence, advice and encouragement to help readers to make their own contribution towards a world where animals are treated with the respect they deserve. Extensive resource listings.

As Director of Animal Aid for the last decade and a campaign organiser for Compassion In World Farming before that, Mark Gold is uniquely qualified to present the truth behind what has become one of the most fiercely debated issues of our age. He is also author of the very successful *Living Without Cruelty* (published 1988).

£7.99 pbk   160pp   1 897766 16 5

Towards a Sustainable Economy

The need for fundamental change

Ted Trainer

A lucid and hard-hitting analysis of the truth about our economic system that explains precisely why a few people are getting richer, most people are getting poorer, and why – if we don't change our ways – we're all heading for global catastrophe. Mass poverty and hunger, unemployment, under-development, waste, armed conflict, resource scarcity and environmental destruction — all are caused by the disastrous flaws in our economy.

Ted Trainer shows how economic growth is seriously mistaken because it ignores finite resource and ecological limits, thereby promoting violence and injustice as well as ecological calamity.

Having invalidated both 'free enterprise capitalism' and 'big state socialism' as viable long-term economic systems, Dr Trainer puts forward an alternative, a Third Way 'conserver society' that includes some of the best elements of the other two. His argument is that an economy for a sustainable world order must involve simpler living standards, a high degree of local economic self-sufficiency and therefore much less transport and travel, a much smaller cash sector of the economy, more cooperative arrangements such as town banks and working bees, and many free goods from Permaculture-designed 'edible landscapes'.

The 'limits to growth' are as real as ever, and we ignore them at our peril.

Ted Trainer's previous books include *Abandon Affluence!* ("Spares no illusions" – *The Ecologist*) and *The Conserver Society* (both Zed Books) and *Developed to Death* (Green Print, now in its third printing).

£10.99   192pp   paperback   1 897766 14 9